FINANCIAL STATEMENTS A$AP!

UNLOCK THE SECRETS TO SMART INVESTMENTS
AND BUSINESS GROWTH

JOHN COUSINS

BizB Press

New York   London

First published by BizB Press 2024

❀ Created with Vellum

LEVEL UP

For more business skills and knowledge check out www.mba-asap.com and sign up for the our newsletter!

INTRODUCTION

Being able to read and understand financial statements is a fundamental skill to understanding how businesses function. Since financial statements are the end product of accounting, understanding them provides the context for understanding accounting. Mastering this skill will help you become a better manager.

Being able to read financial statements will also help you make better investment decisions in the stock market because you will be able to get meaningful information out of an Annual Report or a 10K.

If you are an entrepreneur planning a start up then understanding financial statements is critical for your credibility as you meet with angel investors, bankers, and VCs.

I hope you find this e book helpful as an introduction, refresher, or reference. Email with any comments or questions you have at John@mba-asap.com

I enjoy hearing from and connecting with you!

John Cousins

CHAPTER 1
FINANCIAL STATEMENTS

ACCOUNTING INFORMATION IS PREPARED, organized, and conveyed is in Financial Statements. Financial statements are reports in which accounting information is organized so *users* of financial information have a consistent, quick, and thorough means of reading and understanding what is going on in the business.

There are two basic financial statements: the **Balance Sheet** and the **Income Statement**.

Interested parties need to understand the financial and accounting activities of a business. The Balance Sheet and Income Statement are a formal record of the financial activities of a business. They are presented in a structured manner and in a form that is consistent and easy to understand once you understand the format.

Financial Statements provide a high level view of accounting and a summary of how a business is performing. They provide a quick picture that can be easily compared across businesses and industries. Understanding how to read and analyze a Balance Sheet and Income Statement is a great place to start understanding accounting and finance.

Financial statements are the end product of bookkeeping. Think of financial statements as the destination or goal of bookkeeping and accounting. When you know where you are going and who the audience is, it is easier to make good bookkeeping decisions. When you understand the liquidity, solvency and capital structure of a company you can make good financing and investment decisions.

Financial Statements contain information required to quickly analyze and assess the relative health of a business. A basic understanding of financial statements also provides the high level perspective on the goals of the bookkeeping work and accounting entries. The daily operations of a business are measured in the money that comes in as revenues, the money that goes out as expenses, the money that is retained as profit, the money that is invested in operational assets, and the money that is owed. It's all about the money. Financial statements let you follow the money.

The report that measures these daily operations, of money in and money out over a period of time, is the Income Statement.

———

CHAPTER 2
INCOME STATEMENT

THE INCOME STATEMENT can be summarized as: Revenues less Expenses equals Net Income. The term Net Income simply means Income (Revenues) *net* (less) of Expenses. Net Income is also called Profit or Earnings. Revenues are sometimes called Sales.

You understand this concept intuitively. We always strive to sell things for more than they cost us to make. When you buy a house you hope that it will appreciate in value so you can sell it in the future for more than you paid for it. In order to have a sustainable business model in the long run, the same logic applies. You can't sell things for less than they cost you to make and stay in business for long.

Think of the Income Statement in relation to your monthly personal finances. You have your monthly revenues: in most cases a salary from your job. You apply that monthly income to your monthly expenses: rent or mortgage, car loan, food, gas, utilities, clothes, phone, entertainment, etc. Our goal is to have our expenses be less than our income.

. . .

Over time, and with experience, we become better managers of our personal finances and begin to realize that we shouldn't spend more that we make. We strive to have some money left over at the end of the month that we can set aside and save. What we set aside and save is called **Retained Earnings**.

Some of what we set aside we may **invest** with an eye toward future benefits. We may invest in stocks and bonds or mutual funds, or we may invest in education to expand our future earning and working prospects. This is the same type of money management discipline that is applied in business. It's just a matter of scale. There are a few additional zeros after the numbers on a large company's Income Statement but the idea is the same.

This concept applies to all businesses. **Revenues** are usually from Sales of products or services. **Expenses** are what you spend to support the operations: Salaries, raw materials, manufacturing processes and equipment, offices and factories, consultants, lawyers, advertising, shipping, utilities etc. What is left over is the Net Income or Profit. Again: Revenues – Expenses = Net Income. "Your Income needs to be more than your Outflow or your Upkeep is your Downfall." My Mom used to say that. :)

Net income is either saved in order to smooth out future operations and deal with unforeseen events; or invested in new facilities, equipment, and technology. Or part of the profits can be paid out to the company owners, sometimes called **shareholders** or stockholders, as a **dividend**.

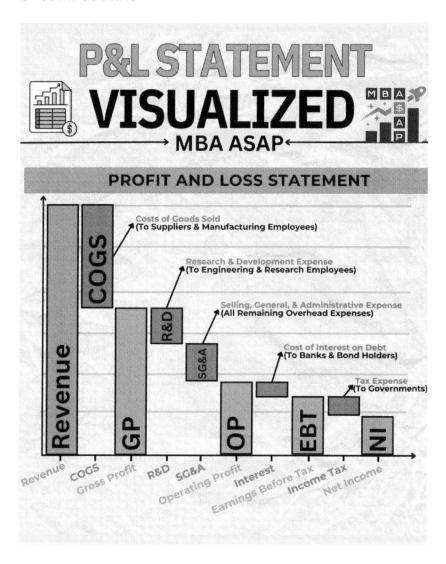

Below is a sample Income Statement to give you a sense of the format and presentation of the numbers.

SAMPLE INCOME STATEMENT

Company X
Income Statement

For Year Ended December 31, 2022
(in thousands)

NET SALES	$ 4,358,100
COST OF SALES	2,738,714
GROSS PROFIT	1,619,386
SELLING AND OPERATING EXPENSES	560,430
GENERAL AND ADMINISTRATIVE EXPENSES	293,729
TOTAL OPERATING EXPENSES	854,159
OPERATING INCOME	765,227
OTHER INCOME	960
GAIN (LOSS) ON FINANCIAL INSTRUMENTS	5,513
(LOSS) GAIN ON FOREIGN CURRENCY	(12,649)
INTEREST EXPENSE	(18,177)
INCOME BEFORE TAXES	740,874
INCOME TAX EXPENSE	257,642
NET INCOME	$ 483,232

Sample Income Statement

The Income Statement is also known as the "profit and loss statement" or "statement of revenue and expense." Business people sometimes use the shorthand term "**P&L**," which stands for profit and loss statement. A manager is said to have "P&L responsibilities" if they run an autonomous division where they make the decisions about marketing, sales, staffing, products, expenses, and strategy. **P & L responsibility** is one of the most important responsibilities of any executive position and involves monitoring the net income after expenses for a department or entire organization, with direct influence on how company resources are allocated.

Income Statement Cheat Sheet

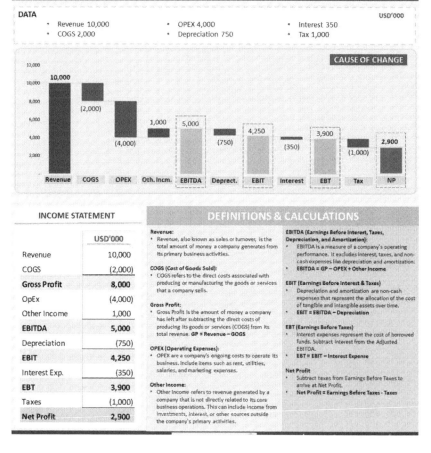

The terms "profits," "earnings" and "net income" all mean the same thing and are used interchangeably.

. . .

Remember: **Income (revenue or sales) – Expenses = Net Income or profit**

Google the term "income statement" and you will see lots of examples of formats and presentations. You will see there is variety depending on the industry and nature of the business but they all follow these basic principles.

———

Income Statement Synonyms

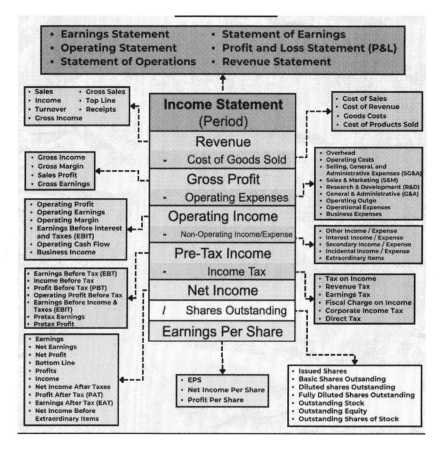

EBITDA
Explained
by Nicolas Boucher

EBITDA stands for:

E	→	Earnings
B	→	Before
I	→	Interest
T	→	Taxes
D	→	Depreciation
A	→	Amortization

What is EBITDA?

It's a financial metric that shows how much money a company makes before taking into account non operational expenses like interest and taxes and non cash expenses like depreciation and amortization.

Why is EBITDA important for Businesses?

EBITDA is important because it gives businesses an idea of **how much money** they're generating from their operations.

This is useful for investors and lenders who want to know **how profitable a company is.**

It's like a **scorecard to know** how much money a company is making.

How is EBITDA calculated?

To calculate EBITDA, you need to start with a company's revenue and subtract its cost of goods sold.

Then, you subtract its operating expenses (like salaries and rent).

EBITDA

In EBITDA, you don't take into consideration these expenses:
Depreciation, Taxes, Interest.

VS

NET INCOME

But the net income is what remains as actual profit after depreciation, interest, taxes are taken in account.

Earnings Before Interest, Taxes, Depreciation, and Amortization

+ Net Income
+ Interest Expense
+ Taxes
+ Depreciation
+ Amortization

} EBITDA

Margin & Markup

MARGIN SHOWS HOW MUCH OF YOUR PRODUCT SALES PRICE YOU KEPT	MARKUP SHOWS HOW MUCH OVER COST YOU'VE SOLD YOUR PRODUCT FOR
$$\frac{(REVENUE - DIRECT\ COST)}{REVENUE}$$	$$\frac{(REVENUE - DIRECT\ COST)}{DIRECT\ COST}$$
## MARGIN %	## MARKUP %

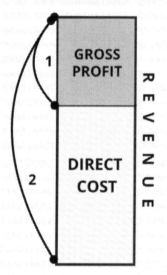

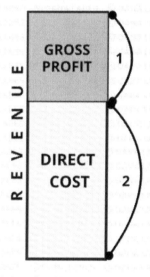

MARGIN = MARKUP/ (1+MARKUP)   MARKUP = MARGIN / (1-MARGIN)

CHAPTER 3
THE BALANCE SHEET

THE BALANCE SHEET can be summarized as: **Assets = Liabilities + Equity**. This is called the accounting equation; memorize it. These three balance sheet segments give the interested reader an idea as to what a company owns (**assets**) and owes (**liabilities**), and the amount invested and accumulated by the owners or shareholders (**equity**).

The Balance Sheet is a snapshot of the financial position of a company at a particular point in time. It is compiled at the end of the year or quarter. It is a summary of the Assets, Liabilities and Equity.

Think of how your home is financed as simple balance sheet. The **asset** is the value of the house. This is determined by an appraisal or sale. The value of your home varies as the market varies. An appraiser takes into account recent sales in the area and adjusts for differences like an extra bedroom or bathroom. An appraisal also takes into account replacement value; how much would it cost to recreate the house with the current costs for materials and labor. The **liability** is the **mortgage** balance and the **equity** (in this case we call it the homeowner's equity) is the difference between the two.

. . .

If the house is worth more than you owe, then you have positive equity. If the mortgage balance is more than the value of the home, then you have negative equity, sometimes called being "upside down" or "underwater".

The same concepts apply to a corporate balance sheet. If the assets are greater than the liabilities then there is positive shareholder's equity. If the liabilities are more than the assets, the company is considered **insolvent**. In this case a company declares bankruptcy.

BALANCE SHEET PRESENTATION

A Balance Sheet is constructed of two basic parts. Assets are listed in a column and totaled at the bottom of the column. Liabilities and Equity are listed in another column with the liabilities section listed above the equity section. Liabilities and Equity are each totaled separately and then together at the bottom. Sometimes these columns are presented in a stacked form with the Asset column on top. And sometimes these columns are presented side by side with the Assets on the left hand side and both Liabilities and Equity on the right hand side.

The Liabilities and Equity show how the Assets are financed. Liabilities and Equity totals in the right hand column must exactly equal the Asset total at the bottom of the left hand column.

When someone talks about the left hand side of the balance sheet, they are referring to assets; if they talk about the right hand side of the balance sheet, they mean liabilities and equity.

. . .

For comparison purposes, the Balance Sheet numbers of the previous year are also usually presented next to this year's numbers. Remember the goal of these Financial Statements is to present the financial information in a clear and meaningful way so interested parties can quickly grasp the performance and status of the enterprise.

According to GAAP, the U.S. accounting standard, assets and liabilities are listed in the order of their liquidity, from short term to long term, as you go down the items listed in each column. Cash is the most liquid asset so it is listed on the top left of the Balance Sheet. Long term debt comes after short term debts in the Liability column and Equity is listed below the Liabilities. Equity is listed below Liabilities because shareholders have a junior claim on the assets of the corporation. In case of a bankruptcy or liquidation of the company, the money collected from the sale of assets goes first to pay the lenders. Any residual money after the lenders are paid off is distributed to the shareholders.

Outsides the United States, the rest of the world presents balance sheet items in the reverse order, from least liquid on top to most liquid at the bottom. The International Accounting Standards are referred to as IAS.

SAMPLE BALANCE SHEET

On the following page you find an example of a Balance Sheet. This is Apple's Balance Sheet from its 10K to give a feel for a real companies reporting. Since they vary in their contents and presentation it is a good idea to take a quick look at a bunch of examples. Google the term "balance sheet" and you will see lots of examples in various formats and presentations.

Apple Inc.
CONSOLIDATED BALANCE SHEETS
(In millions, except number of shares which are reflected in thousands and par value)

	September 26, 2020	September 28, 2019
ASSETS:		
Current assets:		
Cash and cash equivalents	$ 38,016	$ 48,844
Marketable securities	52,927	51,713
Accounts receivable, net	16,120	22,926
Inventories	4,061	4,106
Vendor non-trade receivables	21,325	22,878
Other current assets	11,264	12,352
Total current assets	143,713	162,819
Non-current assets:		
Marketable securities	100,887	105,341
Property, plant and equipment, net	36,766	37,378
Other non-current assets	42,522	32,978
Total non-current assets	180,175	175,697
Total assets	$ 323,888	$ 338,516
LIABILITIES AND SHAREHOLDERS' EQUITY:		
Current liabilities:		
Accounts payable	$ 42,296	$ 46,236
Other current liabilities	42,684	37,720
Deferred revenue	6,643	5,522
Commercial paper	4,996	5,980
Term debt	8,773	10,260
Total current liabilities	105,392	105,718
Non-current liabilities:		
Term debt	98,667	91,807
Other non-current liabilities	54,490	50,503
Total non-current liabilities	153,157	142,310
Total liabilities	258,549	248,028
Commitments and contingencies		
Shareholders' equity:		
Common stock and additional paid-in capital, $0.00001 par value: 50,400,000 shares authorized; 16,976,763 and 17,772,945 shares issued and outstanding, respectively	50,779	45,174
Retained earnings	14,966	45,898
Accumulated other comprehensive income/(loss)	(406)	(584)
Total shareholders' equity	65,339	90,488
Total liabilities and shareholders' equity	$ 323,888	$ 338,516

See accompanying Notes to Consolidated Financial Statements.
Apple Inc. | 2020 Form 10-K

ASSETS AND DEPRECIATION

Assets are listed on the left hand side of the balance sheet. There are liquid assets such as cash, marketable securities, and Accounts Receivable. These are called **Current Assets**. Many assets are long lived items like equipment, vehicles, factories, and machines. These are called **Fixed Assets**. A significant amount of money is spent when fixed assets are purchased. Fixed assets have a shelf life that is significantly longer than the year in which they are purchased. For these reasons fixed assets are **capitalized** at their cost and each year of their proposed useful life a portion of the price is expensed to show how much of the asset was "used" in that year. This concept is called **Depreciation**. It provides a more accurate picture of how the operating assets of a company are contributing to the operations and spreads the expense through the years of its useful life when the asset is contributing to generating revenues.

FIXED ASSETS
LIFE CYCLE MANAGEMENT SYSTEM

Must Have Functionalities
* Integration with other Finance Software – especially AP and GL
* Maintains Audit Trail
* Automatic generation of Asset Number
* Automated depreciation calculations based on different methods
* Ability to define fixed asset categories
* Restriction to select asset categories only from the pre-defined list (user shouldn't be able to define any category during data entry)
* Assign useful life to various categories
* Automatically assign useful life based on asset category
* Split assets entered as bulk assets
* Mass capitalization for more significant projects

Mandatory Fields
* Asset Description
* Purchase Date
* Depreciation start date if it is different from the purchase date
* Asset Category
* Asset location
* Serial Number
* User/Custodian Name
* Asset Tag Number
* Cost value
* Accumulated Depreciation (once the depreciation is calculated)
* NBV

Reporting
* Fixed Assets Register with the minimum following information
  * Asset Description
  * Asset ID/Number
  * Asset Category
  * Asset Location
  * Asset User/Custodian, if any
  * Cost
  * Accumulated Depreciation
  * NBV
* Depreciation schedule with following information:
  * Cost
  * Accumulated Depreciation
  * NBV
  * Useful Life
  * Life Remaining
  * Depreciation start date
  * Depreciation Expense for the period
* Assets Disposal Report
* Assets Movement/Transfer Report
* Depreciation forecast report
* Physical verification reconciliation report

Must Have Options
* Export/Import FA data – necessary for bulk assets upload
* Scalability and Customization – for future growth
* Able to add cost to the same asset in case of additional cost arising at a later date
* Ability to automatically reconcile physical inventory with the FAR
* Able to restrict user access based on the job responsibilities

Nice to Have Options
* Integrity reports if it is interfaced with any other financial system
* Asset Sub-Categories Levels
* Useful life is assigned at the lowest level of the asset category
* Merge assets
* Nice to have fields:
  * Vendor Information
  * Warranty Information
  * Asset Images/Attachments
  * Lease/Rental Information
  * Barcodes
  * Insurance Information
  * Condition of the Asset
  * Asset taken out of service information
  * Notes/Comments

Equipment for Physical Verification
* Barcode Printer
* Barcode Scanners
* Barcode or QR Code Labels
* Asset Tags
* Mobile Devices or Tablets
* Digital Cameras or Smartphone Cameras
* Asset Register Software or Mobile Apps
* GPS Devices

Equipment for RFID Option
* RFID Readers
* RFID Tags or Labels
* RFID Antennas
* RFID Handheld Scanners
* RFID Middleware
* RFID Tags with Sensors
* RFID Portal or Gate Systems
* RFID-Enabled Mobile Devices
* RFID Software or Apps
* RFID Printers

For example if we buy a machine that is assumed to last five years for $50,000 we would record this transaction and list the machine on the Balance Sheet at $50,000 as a Fixed Asset. Each year we would reduce that number by $10,000 of depreciation ($50,000/5). So in the second year the asset would show up as being worth $40,000; $30,000 in the third year and so on. The number shown on the balance sheet is the original asset at cost, less (net of) depreciation. Assets are not listed individually on the Balance Sheet but are aggregated together and shown as a total number.

This is one reason why we need a Cash Flow Statement. The $50,000 would reduce our cash position in the first year and that would show up in the Investment section of the Cash Flow Statement. Each subsequent year, the $10,000 depreciation expense listed in the Income Statement would be added back in the Cash Flow Statement because it was not a cash expense in that year. It was just an accounting expense to keep track of the amount we are allocating to the "use" of the machine.

ASPECT	TANGIBLE ASSETS	INTANGIBLE ASSETS
NATURE	Physical presence; can be seen and touched	Non-physical presence; cannot be seen or touched
EXAMPLES	Buildings Machinery Vehicles Inventory	Trademarks (TM) Patents Copyrights (C) Goodwill
DEPRECIATION/ AMORTIZATION	Depreciated over their useful life	Amortized over their useful life
VALUATION	Generally based on cost or market value	Often based on the income approach or market comparables
FINANCIAL STATEMENT LOCATION	*Balance Sheet*	*Balance Sheet*
LIFESPAN	Typically have a finite lifespan	Can have an indefinite lifespan
RISK OF OBSOLESCENCE	Higher due to physical deterioration or technological advancements	Lower, but can be affected by changes in law, market demand, or technology
COLLATERAL VALUE	Often used as collateral for loans due to physical value	Less commonly used as collateral due to difficulty in valuation
CREATION	Acquired or constructed physically	Created through legal or intellectual effort

AMORTIZATION

Amortization is similar to depreciation.

Depreciation is used for tangible assets and amortization is used for intangible assets such as intellectual property like patents and trademarks. Amortization roughly matches an asset's expense with the revenue it generates. Amortization can also refer to the paying off of debt with a fixed repayment schedule that included both interest and principal in regular installments over a period of time.

These types of non-cash events are what are compensated for in the Operations section of the Cash Flow Statement in order to accurately reconcile the financial statements to how much cash is in the bank. We will discuss the Cash Flow Statement in more detail after we finish talking about the right side of the Balance Sheet: Liabilities and Equity.

LIABILITIES

Liabilities are claims against the company's assets. These claims are categorized as current or non-current. Current liabilities are ones that will come due within the year. Liabilities consist of obligations the enterprise owes to others. Along with Equity, they are how assets are funded. The debt can be to an unrelated third party, such as a bank, or to employees for wages earned but not yet paid. Accounts payable, payroll liabilities, and notes payable are examples of Liabilities.

Both assets and liabilities are categorized as current and non-current. This distinction is essential for the user of the financial statements to perform ratio analysis. We will discuss ratio and other financial statement analysis techniques later in this book.

CURRENT LIABILITIES

Current liabilities are ones the company expects to settle within 12 months of the date on the balance sheet. Income and Assets are used to pay these liabilities. The money can come from revenues generated from sales, or from current assets such as cash in the bank account.

The most common Current Liabilities are accounts payable. Any money a company owes its vendors for supplies or services, or to employees in the form of wages, or the government for taxes is considered a current liability. Most companies accrue payroll and related payroll taxes, which means the company owes them but has not yet paid them. All these types of obligations are acknowledged by the company and are intended to be settled in the relative near term.

Loans due in less than 12 months after the balance sheet date are also current liabilities. For example, a business may need a brief bridge loan in order to meet a payroll expense. Often this is structured as a line of credit (LOC) with the expectation that the LOC will be paid off from the collection of accounts receivable or the sale of inventory.

Current portion of long-term notes payable is also considered a current liability. A long-term note will be paid back in full after that 12-month period. However, you must show the current portion, that which will be paid back in the current operating period, as a current liability.

Unearned revenue is a category that includes money the company has collected from customers but hasn't yet earned by performing the work. The company anticipates completing the tasks and earning the income within 12 months of the date of the balance sheet.

LONG TERM LIABILITIES

Non-current or long-term liabilities are ones the company doesn't expect to be liquidating or settling within 12 months of the balance sheet date. Businesses use debt to finance a portion of their activities and assets. These are structured as loans, notes, or bonds with interest and principal payments over the term. A business is financed by a mixture of debt and equity. This mix is called the capital structure of the company.

· · ·

There are different types of Long Term Debt. They differ primarily by their claim on the assets of the company. This becomes important when a company becomes insolvent and declares bankruptcy. Senior debt is first in line to get paid from the proceeds of the sale of assets. Junior debt has to wait until the senior debt is paid off before it can get its money back. As you can see this makes junior debt more risky because it has a greater chance of not getting paid back in the event of bankruptcy. Because there is more risk, junior debt positions demand a higher interest rate to compensate for taking more risk.

Another financing instrument is Convertible Debt which can be converted into stock.

Stockholders' Equity

Stockholder's Equity, along with liabilities, can be thought of as the funding sources of the company's assets. The stockholders are the owners of the company. The ownership of a corporation is divided into **stock** or shares. There is an amount of shares authorized for the company when is created. This amount of authorized shares can be increased by a vote of the existing shareholders. A corporation raises money by selling shares of stock. The amount of shares issued and sold is called the Shares Outstanding. This represents 100% of the ownership of the corporation. The amount of money raised and the amount of shares issued is tabulated and displayed in the Equity section of the Balance Sheet.

Stockholder's equity is equal to the asset amounts reported on the balance sheet minus the reported liability amounts. Or put another way, Equity is the residual of assets minus liabilities. In order to understand this think of the basic accounting equation:
    Assets = Liabilities + Equity

And rearrange it to solve for Equity

Equity = Assets – Liabilities

In a corporation there may be more than one type of stock issued. These classes of stock will have different rights relative to voting and claims on assets and as such will have different values. In simple terms we can classify stock into two types: Common and Preferred.

COMMON STOCK

Common Stock is the type of stock that forms the ownership of every corporation. Shares of common stock provide evidence of ownership in a corporation. Holders of common stock elect the corporation's directors and share in the distribution of profits of the company via dividends. If the corporation goes bankrupt and liquidates, the secured, or senior, lenders are paid first, followed by unsecured, or junior, lenders, then the preferred stockholders, and lastly the common stockholders.

PREFERRED STOCK

Another financing instrument that corporations can issue in addition to their common stock is preferred stock. **Preferred Stock** is a class of stock that provides for preferential treatment of dividends. The preferred dividend can be thought of like interest on a loan. Preferred stockholders will be paid dividends before the common stockholders receive dividends. These dividends are sometimes paid in stock instead of money.

Both the common and preferred stock accounts are separated into two categories: Par Value and Additional Paid-in Capital or APIC. The bulk of the money is allocated to APIC.

PAR VALUE

The Par Value account is simply a nominal value like one cent and a way to keep track of the amount of shares outstanding. The par value is a small monetary value attributed to each share. It is an arbitrary number, usually $.01. So if the company has 1,000 shares outstanding there would be $100.00 in the par value account. Par Value may also be $0.001. Par Value has no connection to the market value of the share of stock. Think of it as a place holder.

ADDITIONAL PAID-IN CAPITAL (APIC)

The Additional Paid-in Capital (APIC) account is where the amount paid for a share of stock, less the par value, is recorded. When a share of common stock having a par value of $0.01 is issued for $15, the account Common Stock will be credited for $0.01 and the corresponding Additional Paid-in Capital or APIC account will be credited for $14.99 (and Cash will be debited for $15.00).

RETAINED EARNINGS

Retained Earnings is the stockholders' equity account that records and reports the net income of a corporation from its inception until the balance sheet date less the dividends declared from its inception to the date of the balance sheet. This account tracks the profits or losses accumulated since a business was opened. The profits and losses accrue to the shareholders. At the end of each year, the profit or loss calculated on the income statement is used to adjust the value of this account. In an analogy from your personal life, think of Retained Earnings as your savings left over after you have paid all your expenses.

CONTRA ACCOUNTS

A contra account offsets the balance in another, related account with which it is paired. If the related account is an asset account, then a contra asset account is used to offset it with a credit balance. If the related account is a liability or equity account, then a contra liability or equity account is used to offset it with a debit balance. Stockholders' equity accounts normally have credit balances.

Contra equity accounts are a category of equity accounts with debit balances. A debit balance in an owner's equity account is contrary (contra) to an equity account's usual credit balance. An example of a contra stockholders' equity account is **Treasury Stock**. Treasury stock is a corporation's own stock that has been repurchased from stockholders and is being held by the corporation. Because it is stock that is outstanding but not in the hands of shareholders, it needs to be subtracted from the value of the outstanding stockholder's shares in order to properly value the equity. This is the purpose of a contra account. Depreciation is an asset contra account that reduces the value of an asset in a similar way.

We have now discussed the major accounts equity accounts. Some may be named differently but these synonyms represent the same functions. The stockholders' equity section of a corporation's balance sheet will look like this:

STOCKHOLDER'S EQUITY

Paid-in capital
    Common Stock
    Preferred Stock
    Additional Paid-in Capital – Common Stock
    Additional Paid-in Capital – Preferred Stock
    Additional Paid-in Capital – Treasury Stock
    Retained Earnings
    Less: Treasury Stock
    Total Stockholder's Equity

Debt vs Equity

Definition

Debt refers to money borrowed by one entity from another, which must be repaid, typically with interest.

Definition

Equity represents company ownership, typically as shares in a corporation. Investors purchase these shares

Where to find

Where to find

Types of Debt

Long-term debt   Convertible   Line of Credit

Types of Equity

Common Stock   Preferred Stock

Pros of Debt

1. Tax Benefits: Interest payments are tax-deductible, reducing taxable income.
2. Ownership Control: Debt does not dilute existing shareholders' equity stakes.

Pros of Equity

1. No Repayment Obligation: Equity doesn't require repayment like debt does.
2. Access to Additional Funds: Can raise significant capital without increasing debt.

Cons of Debt

1. Financial Risk: Regular interest payments can strain company cash flows.
2. Restrictive Covenants: Debt agreements may limit management's operational flexibility.

Cons of Equity

1. Ownership Dilution: New shares reduce existing shareholders' percentage ownership.
2. Dividend Expectations: Shareholders may expect regular dividend payments.

WORKING CAPITAL

→ **MBA ASAP** ←

Working Capital measures the difference between a company's Current Assets and Current Liabilities.

Balance Sheet (Specific Date)				
Assets			**Liabilities**	
Current Assets (<1 Year)	Cash & Cash Equivalents	Current Liabilities (<1 Year)	Payables & Accrued Expenses	
	Marketable Securities		Short-Term Debt	
	Accounts Receivable		Other Current Liabilities	
	Inventory	Long-Term Liabilities (>1 Year)	Long-Term Debt	
	Other Current Assets		Other Long-Term Liabilities	
Long-Term Assets (>1 Year)	Long-Term Investments	Shareholder Equity	Preferred Stock	
	Fixed Assets		Common Stock & Additional Paid-In Capital	
	Goodwill		Retained Earnings	
	Other Long-Term Assets		Treasury Stock	

Working Capital (also called Net Working Capital), measures a company's liquidity and short-term financial health.

3 WAYS TO CALCULATE NET WORKING CAPITAL

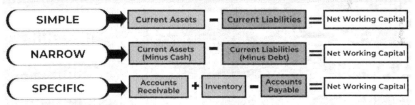

SIMPLE ▶ Current Assets − Current Liabilities = Net Working Capital

NARROW ▶ Current Assets (Minus Cash) − Current Liabilities (Minus Debt) = Net Working Capital

SPECIFIC ▶ Accounts Receivable + Inventory − Accounts Payable = Net Working Capital

BALANCE SHEET
REPORTS | RECONCILIATIONS | ANALYSES | KPIs | RATIOS

	Reconciliation	Report	Analysis	KPI	Ratio
CURRENT ASSETS Cash & Bank	Bank Reconciliation	Petty Cash Reconciliation	Petty Cash Spot Check Report	Daily Cash Position Report	Cash Conversion Cycle (CCC)	Cash Ratio
Accounts Receivable	Accounts Receivable Aging	Bad Debt Provision Reconciliation	Sales Order Backlog Report		Days Sales Outstanding (DSO)	Receivables
Inventory	Physical Inventory Reconciliation	COGS Reconciliation	Slow Moving	Stock Turnover Ratio Report	Inventory	Days Sales of
Prepaid Expenses	Prepaid Expenses Rollforward	Amortization Schedule	Unapplied Prepaid Analysis		Prepaid Expense as a	Turnover Ratio / Prepaid Expense Days
Due from Intercompany	Intercompany Reconciliation	Intercompany Aging Report	Prepaid Expenses Aging Report / Intercompany Elimination Report	Intercompany Interest Analysis	%age of Total Assets Intercompany Receivable Turnover	
FIXED (LONG TERM) ASSETS						
Property, Plant, and Equipment	Fixed Assets Register	Depreciation Reconciliation	Capital Expenditure Report	Maintenance Cost Analysis	Return on Assets (ROA)	Asset Utilization
Intangible Assets	Intangible Assets Register	Amortization Schedule			Return on Intangible Assets	Value as a % of Total Assets
Investments	Investment Portfolio Statement	Fair Value Reconciliation	Investment Income Analysis	Impairment Test Report	Return on Investments (ROI)	Investment Portfolio Diversification Ratio
LIABILITIES AND OWNER'S EQUITY						
CURRENT LIABILITIES						
Accounts Payable	Accounts Payable Aging Report	Vendor Statement Reconciliation	Purchase Order Matching Report	Invoice Accuracy Analysis	Accounts Payable Turnover Ratio	Days Payable Outstanding (DPO)
Advances from Customers	Customer Advances Reconciliation	Unearned Revenue Rollforward Interest Expense	Customer Deposit Analysis	Sales Contract Compliance Report	Advances as a % of Revenue	Customer Advance Turnover Ratio
Short-Term Loans	Loan Amortization Schedule	Reconciliation	Loan Covenant Adherence Report		Coverage Ratio	Interest Coverage Ratio
Income Taxes Payable	Income Tax Reconciliation	Deferred Tax Asset/Liability	Tax Compliance Checklist	Tax Provision Analysis	Effective Tax Rate	Tax Liability Ratio
Accrued Expenses	Accrual Reconciliation	Accrued Expenses Rollforward	Accrued Liabilities Aging Report	Expense Variance Analysis	Accrued Liability Turnover	
Deferred Revenue	Deferred Revenue Reconciliation	Deferred Revenue Schedule	Analysis	Deferred Revenue Aging Report	Revenue Renewal Rate	Deferred Revenue as a % of T. Revenue
Due to Intercompany	Intercompany Reconciliation	Intercompany Aging Report	Cross-Border Tax Analysis	Transfer Pricing Compliance Report	Intercompany Payable Turnover	Intercompany Payable Days
LONG TERM LIABILITIES						
Long-Term Debt	Long-Term Debt Schedule	Debt Covenant Compliance Report	Debt Maturity Profile	Debt-to-Equity Analysis	Debt Service Coverage Ratio	Debt-to-Capitalization Ratio
Deferred Income Tax	Deferred Income Tax Reconciliation	Effective Tax Rate Analysis			Tax Efficiency Ratio	
OWNER'S EQUITY						
Owner's Equity	Statement of Changes in Equity	Equity Dilution Impact Report	Dividend Declaration Analysis	Equity Rollforward	Return on Equity (ROE)	Earnings Retention Ratio
Retained Earnings	Retained Earnings Reconciliation	Dividend Reconciliation	Profitability Trend Analysis	Earnings Per Share (EPS) Calculation	Dividend Payout Ratio	Retained Earnings Growth Rate

How to Analyze
a Balance Sheet

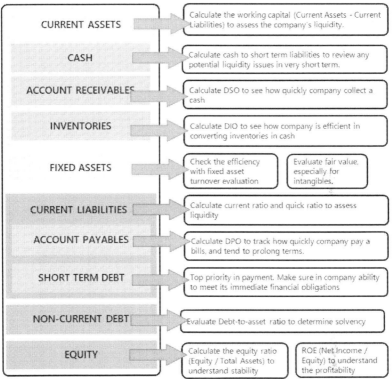

CURRENT ASSETS	Calculate the working capital (Current Assets - Current Liabilities) to assess the company's liquidity.
CASH	Calculate cash to short term liabilities to review any potential liquidity issues in very short term.
ACCOUNT RECEIVABLES	Calculate DSO to see how quickly company collect a cash
INVENTORIES	Calculate DIO to see how company is efficient in converting inventories in cash
FIXED ASSETS	Check the efficiency with fixed asset turnover evaluation / Evaluate fair value, especially for intangibles.
CURRENT LIABILITIES	Calculate current ratio and quick ratio to assess liquidity
ACCOUNT PAYABLES	Calculate DPO to track how quickly company pay a bills, and tend to prolong terms.
SHORT TERM DEBT	Top priority in payment. Make sure in company ability to meet its immediate financial obligations
NON-CURRENT DEBT	Evaluate Debt-to-asset ratio to determine solvency
EQUITY	Calculate the equity ratio (Equity / Total Assets) to understand stability / ROE (Net Income / Equity) to understand the profitability

Make sure you do this in ratio analysis

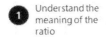 **1** Understand the meaning of the ratio

 2 Result interpretation

 **3** Compare with last period, budget and industry peers

 4 Action plan

CHAPTER 4
CASH FLOW STATEMENT

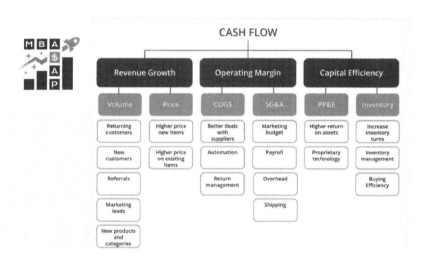

BESIDES THE INCOME Statement and the Balance Sheet, there is a third financial statement called the **Cash Flow Statement**. The Cash Flow Statement reconciles the Income Statement with the actual cash position of the company (the balance in the bank account) by adding and subtracting revenues and expenses that were properly recorded on the Income Statement, but are non-cash events. Depreciation and changes in Accounts Receivable are examples of non-cash events. This reconciled bank account balance is the number that then is used for the Cash account at the top of the asset column on the Balance Sheet. This is important. This is how the financial statements are interconnected.

The need for a Cash Flow Statement arises from Accrual Accounting where we book items like Receivables and Payables and Depreciation in order to provide a more accurate picture of the operations of a company by matching revenues and expenses. These "non-cash" transactions distort the Income Statement relative to how much cash actually came in and went out of the company and how much is actually in the bank. The Operations portion of the Cash Flow Statement reconciles these differences.

Besides **Operations**, there are two other parts of the Cash Flow Statement that follow the Operations portion: **Investing** and **Financing**. The Investing section shows the money that was spent on capital equipment items that don't show up as expenses on the Income Statement because they have been capitalized as Assets. The Financing section primarily shows money that has come into the company through the sale of stock or the proceeds of a loan.

The concepts behind the Cash Flow Statement are relatively nuanced and may seem a bit confusing to someone familiarizing themselves with the basic principles of accounting for the first time. As you read and work with financial statements, the different aspects of the Cash Flow Statement will become clear.

Cash Flow Statement Synonyms

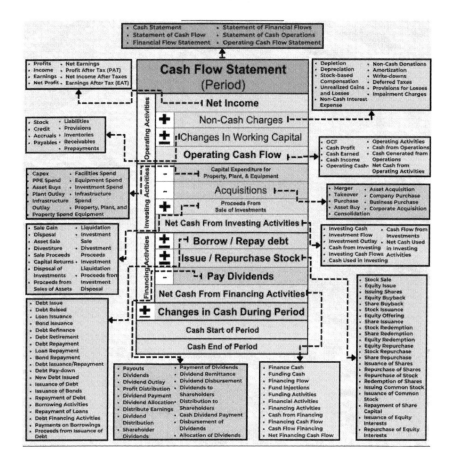

Sample Cash Flow Statement

On the following page you find an example of a simple Cash Flow Statement. Since they vary in their contents and presentation it is a good idea to take a quick look at a bunch of examples. Google the term "Cash Flow Statement" and you will see lots of examples in various formats and presentations.

Example Corporation
Statement of Cash Flows
For the year ended December 31, 2021

Cash flows from operating activities	$230,000
Net income	
Adjustments to reconcile net income to net cash	
provided by operating activities:	
Depreciation and amortization	63,000
Loss on sale of equipment	15,000
Changes in current assets and liabilities:	
Increase in accounts receivable	(21,000)
Decrease in prepaid expenses	3,000
Decrease in accounts payable	(28,000)
Net cash provided by operating activities	262,000
Cash flows from investing activities	
Capital expenditures	(300,000)
Proceeds from sale of equipment	40,000
Net cash used for investing activities	(260,000)
Cash flows from financing activities	
Proceeds from issuing debt	200,000
Dividends paid	(110,000)
Net cash provided by financing activities	90,000
Net increase in cash during the year	**92,000**
Cash at the beginning of the year	101,000
Cash at the end of the year	$193,000

HOW TO ANALYZE A
CASH FLOW STATEMENT

What is a Cash Flow Statement?

- A cash flow statement shows you how much cash goes in and out a company over a certain period
- The purpose of this statement is to track how much cash is moving through a business
- You want to invest in companies that generate cash and manage their cash position well

Structure of a Cash Flow Statement:

- Every cash flow statement consists of 3 parts:
    1. Cash Flow from Operating Activities
    2. Cash Flow from Investing Activities
    3. Cash Flow from Financing Activities

Cash Flow from Operating Activities:

- This section shows all cash the company generated from its normal business activities
- It shows you all the cash a company earned from selling its normal products and/or services
- The Cash Flow from Operating Activities is comparable to net income, but it filters out a few income and expense posts that didn't cause actual cash to enter or exit the company
- fx Cash Flow from Operating Activities = net income + non-cash charges +/- changes in working capital

Cash Flow from Investing Activities:

- The Cash Flow from Investing Activities gives you an overview about the company's investment related income and expenditures
- The Cash Flow from Investing Activities consists of 3 major parts:
    1. Capital expenditures (CAPEX)
    2. Mergers & Acquisitions
    3. Marketable securities
- fx Cash Flow from Investing Activities = Sale of marketable securities + divestments - CAPEX - Mergers & Acquisitions - purchase of marketable securities

Cash Flow from Financing Activities:

- Measures the cash movements between a company and its owners (shareholders) and its debtors (bondholders)
- This section gives you an insight about how the company is financing its business activities
- fx Cash Flow from Financing Activities = Debt issuance + issuance of new stocks - dividends - debt repayments - share buybacks

Changes in cash balance:

- Finally, you can calculate the total changes in the cash balance
- fx Cash at the end of the year = Cash at the beginning of the year + CF from Operating Activities + CF from Investing Activities + CF from Financing Activities

CHAPTER 5
FINANCIAL STATEMENT INTERCONNECTIONS AND FLOW

THE THREE FINANCIAL Statements are interconnected and the numbers flow through them. Basically you start a year with a Balance Sheet showing the financial position at the beginning of the period; next you have the Income Statement that shows the operations during the year period, and then a balance Sheet at the end of the year. The Cash Flow reconciles the cash position starting from the Net Income number at the bottom of the Income Statement. The cash number calculated from the Cash Flow Statement is added to the cash from the beginning Balance Sheet. This number needs to match the actual cash in the bank and is used as the Cash account balance at the top right (Asset column) of the end of year (EOY) Balance Sheet. The Net Income number from the Income Statement is then added to the Retained Earnings number in the Equity section (left hand side) of the end of year (EOY) Balance Sheet. If this is done correctly, all the numbers should reconcile and the Assets will be equal to the Liabilities and Equity of the EOY Balance Sheet.

Think of it as a system of two Balance Sheets acting as book-ends for the Income Statement. And the Cash Flow Statement used to reconcile the Net Income (or Loss) at the bottom of the Income Statement with the amount of cash actually in the bank. This process accounts for every penny that has come in and gone out of a company during the period. Understanding these three financial statements will allow you to assess the financial health, viability and prospects of any company, and make rational fact based investment decisions.

This section, though short, ties together the functionality of the financial statements. This might be an "aha" moment for you. It was for me when I finally realized how this all fit and worked together. Understanding this conceptual big picture of accounting will provide a context to keep you from ever getting lost in the details.

———

How Financial Statements Link

— Increases — Reduces — No Change — Opposite

INCOME STATEMENT		
Account	Year 1	Year 2
Revenue	$100,000	$120,000
Cost of Goods Sold	($50,000)	($55,000)
Gross Profit	$50,000	$65,000
Operating Expenses	$25,000	$30,000
Depreciation	$10,000	$10,000
Operating Profit	$15,000	$25,000
Other Income/Expense	$5,000	$5,000
Taxes	($5,000)	($7,500)
Net Income	$15,000	$22,500

BALANCE SHEET		
Account	Year 1	Year 2
Cash	$70,000	$7,500
Receivables	$25,000	$20,000
Inventory	$10,000	$15,000
Total Current Assets	$105,000	$42,500
Property, Plant & Equipment	$140,000	$180,000
Total Long-Term Assets	$140,000	$180,000
Total Assets	$245,000	$222,500
Payables	$30,000	$20,000
Short-Term Debt	$10,000	$0
Current Liabilities	$40,000	$20,000
Long-Term Debt	$100,000	$75,000
Long-Term Liabilities	$100,000	$75,000
Shareholder's Equity	$105,000	$127,500
Total Liabilities + Equity	$245,000	$222,500

CASH FLOW STATEMENT		
Account	Year 1	Year 2
Net Income	$15,000	$22,500
Depreciation	$10,000	$10,000
(+/-) Inventory	($10,000)	($5,000)
(+/-) Receivables	($25,000)	$5,000
(+/-) Payables	$30,000	($10,000)
Operating Cash Flow	$20,000	$22,500
Capital Expenditures	($150,000)	($50,000)
Investing Cash Flow	($150,000)	($50,000)
Changes in Debt	$110,000	($35,000)
Changes in Shares	$0	$0
Dividends	($10,000)	$0
Financing Cash Flow	$100,000	($35,000)
Change in Cash	($30,000)	($62,500)

CHAPTER 6
THE ROLE OF AUDITORS

AS PER THE SEC requirements and regulations, in order to be eligible to be traded on a stock exchange, a publicly traded company's financials must be prepared by the company and then reviewed and audited by an outside Certified Public Accountant (CPA).

Many investors in private companies also require audited financials in order to ensure that the accounting practices and the financial statement presentation is prepared fairly and transparently.

WHAT IS AN AUDITOR?

The auditing process entails reviewing the financial statements prepared and drafted by the company to make sure they conform to GAAP and other rules. The auditors also "test" the numbers by requesting and reviewing supporting documentation such as invoices, checks, bills, and contracts. They send letters to the company's banks to confirm bank balances and contact lawyers the company has worked with to confirm that there are no latent liabilities or law suits pending that have not been disclosed.

THE AUDITING PROCESS

In any company there are strong temptations to commit fraud. People who run companies have the power to exploit financial information for personal gain. For publicly traded companies annual auditing is a legal requirement and investors of many privately held companies, including their bankers, also require annual audited financial statements.

The audit process is designed to protect against misrepresenting financial information to improve results, avoid taxation, hide fraud, or not report latent liabilities. Audits are a process of gaining information about the financial systems and the financial records of a company.

Financial audits are performed to ascertain the validity and reliability of accounting processes and information, as well as to provide an assessment of the company's internal control system. Audits are carried out by a third party impartial accounting team led by an accountant that is certified as a CPA.

To work on other company's financials you must be a CPA. In the United States a CPA will have passed the Uniform Certified Public Accountant Examination and met additional state education and experience requirements for membership in their state's professional accounting body. You don't have to be a CPA to work for a company internally as an employee in accounting or finance.

Since the auditor cannot feasibly know or discover everything about a company, an audit seeks to provide reasonable assurance that the financial statements are free from material error. Test work and sampling of documents is performed in audits as a way to statistically confirm the likelihood that the accounting has been done properly by the company. A set of financial statements are understood to be 'true and fair' when they are deemed free of material misstatements. The auditor confirms this in their opinion letter that precedes the financials in the final and finished presentation. The opinion given on financial statements depends on the audit evidence obtained. You find the opinion letter at the beginning of the audited financial statements.

———

CHAPTER 7
GAAP AND IFSR

GAAP IS short for Generally Accepted Accounting Principles. These are the rules and accounting principles that have been adopted by the accounting profession in the United States. The rest of the world has adopted a different set of standards called IFSR. IFSR stands for International Financial Reporting Standards. It is the accounting standard used in more than 110 countries, but not in the United States. Both standards intend to capture and represent the economics of accounting transactions as accurately and clearly as possible.

The fact that there are two different accounting frameworks in the world creates complexities that are a problem for users of accounting information and a burden to international companies. International companies must keep two sets of accounting records and provide two completely different sets of audited financial statements. That ends up being a cumbersome and expensive amount of extra work. Although there has been an effort to harmonize the two standards into one universal standard, they have not arrived at one yet.

GAAP VS NON-GAAP ACCOUNTING

→ MBA ASAP ←

	GAAP	Non-GAAP
Audited?	Yes	No
Standardized?	Yes	No
Stock-Based Compensation	Included	Usually Excluded
Non-Recurring Charges • Acquisition Expenses • Currency Movements • Early Debt Redemption Costs • Fines/Penalties • Litigation • Pension • Relocation Expenses • Restructuring Charges • Unusual Taxes	Included	Usually Excluded
Paper Gains/Losses On Investments	Included	Usually Excluded
EBITDA?	No	Yes
Profits Usually Look	Worse	Better

CHAPTER 8
FINANCIAL STATEMENT ANALYSIS

INTRODUCTION

THE LAUNCHING PLACE for Corporate Finance is the ability to read and understand Financial Statements.

The next step is the analysis of financial statements and subsequent assumptions and projections based on that analysis. Financial statement analysis is the process of analyzing a company's financial statements and comparing the analysis across companies and industries to make better operating and investing decisions.

This analysis method involves specific techniques for evaluating and quantifying risk, performance, financial health, and the future prospects of an enterprise.

We can look at the performance of a particular company over time, such as year-to-year results. This type is called Horizontal Analysis.

· · ·

And we can look at various performance characteristics within a single time period. This is called Vertical Analysis.

We can create metrics across an industry segment as an average value to compare our company against. This analysis is called Benchmarking.

We can also aggregate up different industry groups and see how they perform relative to each other. This type of analysis can help gauge where to allocate investment dollars in a portfolio. It can also be used to see how a management team is performing relative to its competition.

Various stakeholders analyze and scrutinize financial statements, including debt and equity investors, government agencies and taxing authorities, and management decision-makers. It is what credit analysts do.

These stakeholders have different interests and apply a variety of different techniques to meet their needs. For example, some equity investors are more interested in the long-term earnings power of the organization and the sustainability and growth of dividend payments.

Some equity investors, like hedge funds, may be looking for latent risks and pitfalls in order to capitalize on a short position. This screening means they are looking for companies about to collapse.

Creditors want to ensure that interest and principal on the organization's debt securities can be paid on time and when due. Banks and commercial lenders use financial statement analysis as part of their credit analysis to determine whether or not to make loans and lend.

Ratings Agencies such as Moody's, Standard and Poors, and Fitch perform financial statement analysis in order to rate the risk and creditworthiness of companies and their debt.

Managers use it to see how their company is performing relative to historical performance, their targets, and industry.

Techniques of financial statement analysis include fundamental analysis, the use of financial ratios, and DuPont analysis.

Analysis methods are performed horizontally or vertically across a company.

In order to project future performance, historical information is used combined with assumptions about the prospects for the company and the future economic environment. This stream of profits from future years is used to calculate a business's value. Calculating the present value of expected future cashflows is the foundational concept of Business Valuation and Corporate Finance.

Before we get into the nitty-gritty of these techniques, let's start with a historical overview of how financial statement analysis developed and has evolved.

HISTORY OF FINANCIAL STATEMENT ANALYSIS

The stock market crash in October 1929 was a catastrophic event that led to the Great Depression and worldwide economic strife. It also led to social unrest and political turmoil. These events called into question the viability of Capitalism and Democracy as unsettling systemic flaws were exposed, and many people suffered.

A major basis of the problem was that many companies that traded on the stock market did not provide meaningful information about the state of their business. There were no financial statements to review. There was no transparency.

In order to clean up the mess and maintain investor confidence in the stock market, the Roosevelt administration created the Securities and Exchange Commission (SEC) to regulate and oversee the stock market.

Roosevelt needed someone to run the SEC who knew all the dirty tricks of the stock market so they could effectively identify and combat abuse. The man who rose to the occasion was Joseph P. Kennedy, John F. Kennedy's father, a famous stock manipulator and patriot.

Part of the SEC's new rules was that every traded company had to have financial statements prepared by an outside third-party auditing firm under a rigorous set of accounting rules called GAAP, Generally Accepted Accounting Principles.

These financial statements, along with disclosures about the operations, had to be filed and made publicly available through the SEC every year.

· · ·

That document is called a **10K**. This kind of disclosure and transparency allows investors and the public to understand a company's operations and prospects and decide whether to invest.

This set of regulations seems obvious and eminently sensible now, but it was bold, brilliant, and a revelation at the time.

Fundamental analysis, a system of analyzing this newly available information, emerged almost immediately.

To this day, the 10K is the primary document, and fundamental analysis is the toolset for stock market analysis and corporate investment decision-making.

FUNDAMENTAL ANALYSIS

The SEC and financial reporting regulations were instituted in two legislations: the '33 Act and the '34 Act.

Benjamin Graham and David Dodd first published their influential book "Security Analysis" in 1934. Warren Buffett is a well-known disciple of Graham and Dodd's philosophy.

The Graham and Dodd approach is referred to as Fundamental Analysis and includes Economic analysis, Industry analysis, and Company analysis.

Company Analysis is the primary realm of financial statement analysis. Based on these three analyses, the value of the security is determined. Fundamental analysis is how bankers, analysts, and investors make long-term investment decisions.

Their book has gone through many revisions and editions and is available in a recently revised edition. Try to check it out, especially if you want to be like Warren. Another proponent of Graham and Dodd is Bill Ackman, the American hedge fund manager. He is the founder and CEO of Pershing Square Capital Management. Bill is also a billionaire.

Here is the information on the book:

Dodd, David; Graham, Benjamin (1998). Security Analysis. John Wiley & Sons, Inc. ISBN 0-07-013235-6.

HORIZONTAL AND VERTICAL ANALYSIS

Horizontal analysis compares financial information over time, typically from past financial statements such as the income statement.

When comparing this past information, we look for variations of particular line items such as higher or lower earnings, sales revenues, or specific expenses.

Horizontal analysis is used to look for trends that can be extrapolated to predict future performance. But remember, past performance is not always a good predictor of future performance.

Vertical analysis is a proportional analysis performed on financial statements. It is ratio analysis. Line items of interest on the financial statement are listed as a percentage of another line item. For example, on an income statement, each line item will be listed as a percentage of Sales.

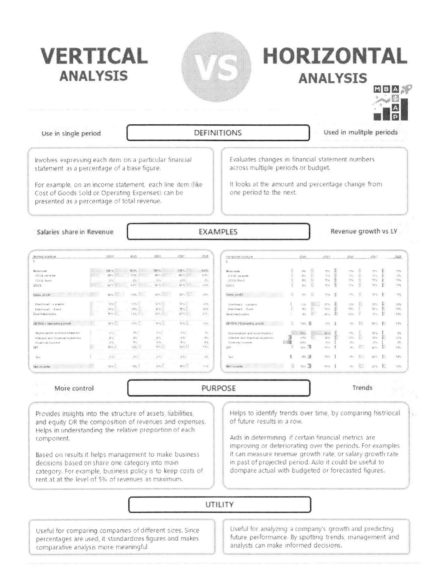

FINANCIAL RATIOS

Financial ratios are powerful tools for assessing a company's upside, downside, and risk.

. . .

There are four main categories of ratios: liquidity, profitability, activity, and leverage. These are typically analyzed over time and across competitors in an industry. Using ratios "normalizes" the numbers to compare companies in apples-to-apples terms.

LIQUIDITY AND SOLVENCY

Solvency and liquidity both refer to a company's financial health and viability. Solvency refers to an enterprise's capacity to meet its long-term financial commitments. Liquidity refers to an enterprise's ability to pay short-term obligations. Liquidity also measures how quickly assets can be sold to raise cash.

A solvent company owns more than it owes. It has a positive net worth and is carrying a manageable debt load. A company with adequate liquidity may have enough cash to pay its bills but may still be heading for financial disaster. In this case a company meets liquidity standards by is not solvent. Healthy companies are both solvent and possess adequate liquidity.

Liquidity ratios are used to determine whether a company has enough current asset capacity to pay its bills and meet its obligations in the foreseeable future (current liabilities).

Solvency ratios measure how quickly a company can turn its assets into cash if it experiences financial difficulties or is threatened with bankruptcy.

Both measure different aspects of if and how long a company can pay its bills and remain in business.

. . .

The current ratio and the quick ratio are two common liquidity ratios. The current ratio is current assets/current liabilities and measures how much liquidity (cash) is available to address current liabilities (bills and other obligations).

The quick ratio is (current assets – inventories) / current liabilities. The quick ratio measures a company's ability to meet its short-term obligations based on its most liquid assets and excludes inventories from its current assets. It is also known as the "acid-test ratio."

The solvency ratio is used to examine the ability of a business to meet its long-term obligations. Lenders and bankers most commonly use the ratio. The ratio compares cash flows to liabilities. The solvency ratio calculation involves the following steps:

• All non-cash expenses are added back to after-tax net income. This approximates the amount of cash flow generated by the business. You can find the numbers to add back in the Operations section of the Cash Flow Statement.

• Add together all short-term and long-term obligations. This is the Total Liabilities number on the Balance Sheet. Then divide the estimated cash flow figure by the liabilities total.

The formula for the ratio is:

(Net after-tax income + Non-cash expenses)/(Short-term liabilities + Long-term liabilities)

A higher percentage indicates an increased ability to support the liabilities of a business over the long term.

. . .

Remember that estimations made over a long term are inherently inaccurate. Many variables can impact the ability to pay over the long term. Using any ratio to estimate solvency must be taken with a grain of salt.

Altman Z Score

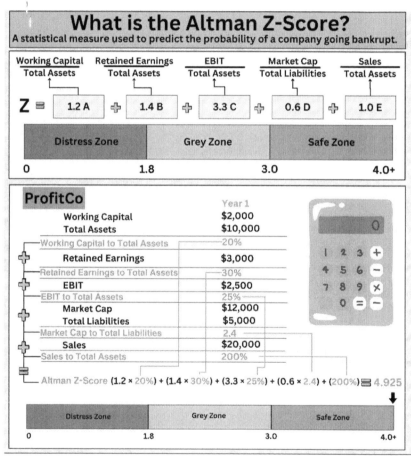

PROFITABILITY RATIOS

Profitability ratios are ratios that help discern how profitable a company is. To be profitable, a company has to cover costs. The breakeven point and the gross profit ratio address the dynamics of cost coverage in different ways. The breakeven point calculates how much cash a company must generate to break even with its operating costs.

The gross profit ratio equals (revenue - the cost of goods sold)/revenue. This ratio provides a quick snapshot of expected revenue that can be applied to the overhead expenses and fixed operations costs.

Some additional examples of profitability ratios are profit margin, return on assets, and return on Equity. The higher the value in these ratios, the more profitable a company is.

A higher value relative to a competitor's ratio or the same ratio from a previous period indicates that the company is performing relatively well and going in the right direction.

Return on Equity
Return on Equity (ROE) = Net Income / Average Shareholders' Equity

ROCE

ROCE = RETURN ON CAPITAL EMPLOYED

What is ROCE?

A ratio that measures how efficiently a company uses its equity and debt to generate profits.

Return on Capital Employed =

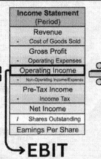

÷

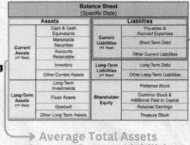

↳ **EBIT**

→ Average Total Assets
- Average Current Liabilities ←

When To Use ROCE

When comparing the performance of companies in the same industry.

PROS	CONS
• Broader measure of capital efficiency. • Simple to calculate and understand. • Useful for capital-intensive industries.	• Can be skewed by high debt levels. • Neglects timing of cash flow. • Not reliable when comparing companies in different industries.

BE AWARE OF ⚠

- Inconsistencies in definition
- Sensitivity to short-term fluctuations
- High debt levels distorting results

DuPont Formula

RETURN ON EQUITY EXPLAINED

- Return on Equity is a performance measure to analyze returns for owners & investors.
- The formula is Net Income (Income Statement) divided by Equity (Balance Sheet)
- The DuPont Formula breaks down Return on Equity into its individual components for analysis.

DUPONT FORMULA

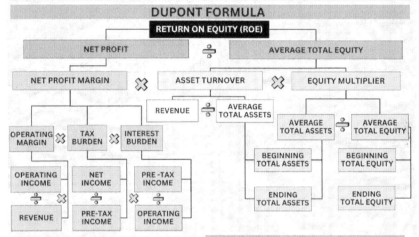

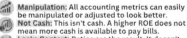

DUPONT FORMULA EXPLAINED

- Return on Equity is Net Profit divided by Equity.
- Dupont Formula breaks out Net Profit and Equity into multiple components.
- In the formula above, everything cancels out except for Net Income and Equity.

Example: Operating Income is in the Top of the Operating Margin and Bottom of Interest Burden Ratio.

Result: Operating Income is canceled out. Only Net Income and Total Equity will remain!

THE THREE DRIVERS	DOWNSIDE
1 Operating Efficiency: highlighted by the net profit margin, or net income / revenue 2 Asset Efficiency: measured by the asset turnover ratio, or revenue / total assets 3 Financial Leverage: measured by the equity multiplier formula, or total assets / total equity	Manipulation: All accounting metrics can easily be manipulated or adjusted to look better. Not Cash: This isn't cash. A higher ROE does not mean more cash is available to pay bills. Lacks Context: Ratios are the result. It doesn't give a why.

ROCE | ROE | ROA | ROIC

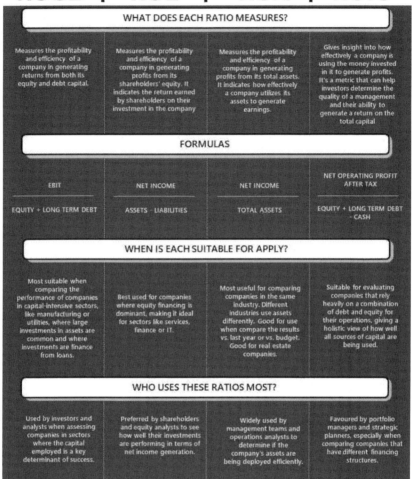

WHAT DOES EACH RATIO MEASURES?			
Measures the profitability and efficiency of a company in generating returns from both its equity and debt capital.	Measures the profitability and efficiency of a company in generating profits from its shareholders' equity. It indicates the return earned by shareholders on their investment in the company	Measures the profitability and efficiency of a company in generating profits from its total assets. It indicates how effectively a company utilizes its assets to generate earnings.	Gives insight into how effectively a company is using the money invested in it to generate profits. It's a metric that can help investors determine the quality of a management and their ability to generate a return on the total capital

FORMULAS			
EBIT	NET INCOME	NET INCOME	NET OPERATING PROFIT AFTER TAX
EQUITY + LONG TERM DEBT	ASSETS - LIABILITIES	TOTAL ASSETS	EQUITY + LONG TERM DEBT - CASH

WHEN IS EACH SUITABLE FOR APPLY?			
Most suitable when comparing the performance of companies in capital-intensive sectors, like manufacturing or utilities, where large investments in assets are common and where investments are finance from loans.	Best used for companies where equity financing is dominant, making it ideal for sectors like services, finance or IT.	Most useful for comparing companies in the same industry. Different industries use assets differently. Good for use when compare the results vs. last year or vs. budget. Good for real estate companies.	Suitable for evaluating companies that rely heavily on a combination of debt and equity for their operations, giving a holistic view of how well all sources of capital are being used.

WHO USES THESE RATIOS MOST?			
Used by investors and analysts when assessing companies in sectors where the capital employed is a key determinant of success.	Preferred by shareholders and equity analysts to see how well their investments are performing in terms of net income generation.	Widely used by management teams and operations analysts to determine if the company's assets are being deployed efficiently.	Favoured by portfolio managers and strategic planners, especially when comparing companies that have different financing structures.

Earnings per Share

Earnings per share (EPS) is the portion of the company's profit that is allocated to each outstanding share of common.

· · ·

Earnings per share is an excellent indicator of the profitability of any organization, and it is one of the most widely used measures of profitability.

ACTIVITY RATIOS

Activity ratios are calculated to show how well management is doing in managing the company's resources. Activity ratios measure company sales relative to another asset account.

The most common asset accounts used are accounts receivable, inventory, and total assets. Since most companies have a lot of resources tied up in accounts receivable, inventory, and working capital, these accounts are used as denominators of the most common activity ratios.

Accounts Receivable

Accounts receivable (AR) is the total amount of money due to a company for products or services sold on a credit account. The length of time until AR is collected is critical because that expected revenue must be financed in some way.

The accounts receivable turnover shows how rapidly a company collects what is owed to it and indicates the liquidity of the receivables.

Accounts Receivable Turnover = Total Credit Sales/Average Accounts Receivable

The average collection period in days is equal to 365 days divided by the Accounts Receivable Turnover. This is another ratio that helps gain insight into AR collection:

. . .

Average Collection Period = 365 Days/Accounts Receivable Turnover

Analysts frequently use the average collection period to measure the effectiveness of a company's ability to collect payments from its credit customers. The average collection period should be less than the company's credit terms to its customers.

Inventory

A significant indicator of profitability is the ability to manage inventory. Inventory is money and resources invested that do not earn a return until the product is sold.

The longer inventory sits, the less profitable a company can be. A higher inventory turnover ratio indicates more demand for products, better cash management, and also the reduced risk of inventory obsolescence.

The best measure of inventory utilization is the inventory turnover ratio. It is calculated as either the total annual sales, or the cost of goods sold (COGS), divided by the cost of inventory.

Inventory Turnover = Total Annual Sales or Cost of Goods Sold/Average Inventory

Using the cost of goods sold in the numerator can provide a more accurate indicator of inventory turnover because it allows a more direct comparison with other companies. Different companies have different markups for the sale price, which can obscure apples-to-apples comparisons.

The average inventory cost is usually used in the denominator to compensate for seasonal differences.

LEVERAGE RATIOS

Leverage ratios analyze the degree to which a company uses debt to finance its operations and assets. The debt-to-equity ratio is the most common. This ratio is calculated as:

(Long-term debt + Short-term debt + Leases)/Equity

Companies with high debt ratios must have steady and predictable revenue streams to service that debt. Companies whose revenues fluctuate and are less predictable should rely more on Equity in their capital structure.

Leverage also has obvious implications for solvency.

Startups rely almost entirely on Equity as they have no revenues or very uncertain revenues that can service debt.

DUPONT ANALYSIS

The DuPont Corporation developed DuPont analysis in the 1920s as a tool to assess their investments across their various companies and operations.

· · ·

As an early conglomerate, they needed a tool to assess the relative performance of varied businesses to decide where and how to allocate resources. It has been widely adopted as a managerial and investment tool.

WHAT DRIVES ROE?

DuPont Analysis analyzes **Return on Equity** by deconstructing it into its main drivers.

DuPont Analysis is an expression that breaks Return on Equity (ROE) into three parts.

The basic formula is:

ROE = (Profit margin)*(Asset turnover)*(Equity multiplier) = (Net Income/Sales)*(Sales/Assets)*(Assets/Equity) = (Net Income/Equity)

The three constituent parts are:
- **Profitability**: measured by profit margin
- **Operating efficiency**: measured by asset turnover
- **Financial leverage**: measured by equity multiplier

DuPont analysis enables you to understand the source of superior (or inferior) returns by comparison with companies in similar industries or between industries. It also provides a deeper level of understanding by parsing apart the significant variables and drivers of Return on Equity. And ROE is undoubtedly a metric that equity investors (stock investors) find essential.

WORKING CAPITAL

Working Capital is a term used to describe the amount of money and liquid assets available and required to operate a business. It is a financial metric that represents operating liquidity.

Working capital is the difference between current assets and current liabilities. Working capital is part of operating capital, along with fixed assets such as plant and equipment. Working capital management involves managing inventories, accounts receivable, accounts payable, and cash.

Current assets and current liabilities include three accounts that are of particular importance. These accounts represent the areas of the business where managers have the most direct impact and influence:
- Accounts receivable (current asset)
- Inventory (current assets), and
- Accounts payable (current liability)

Short-term loans and the current portion of long-term debt (payable within 12 months) are also critical because they represent short-term claims on current assets and are usually secured by long-term assets.

Bank loans and lines of credit are common types of short-term debt.

An increase in net working capital indicates that the business has either increased current assets or has decreased current liabilities. Financing and managing working capital is a major operating challenge, especially for rapidly growing companies.

MANAGING WORKING CAPITAL

Receivables and inventory are usually financed with a line of credit (revolving debt like a credit card). Managing receivables aims to ensure that all your customers pay and that they pay on time; you need that cash in the door!

Accounts Receivables turnover is a ratio we discussed earlier that indicates the timeliness of credit sales being paid.

Managing inventories means keeping inventories from building up. You do this by monitoring sales, manufacturing activity, and the Inventory turnover ratio.

You want enough inventories to accommodate a spike in sales, but you also want to avoid having too much inventory that you can't unload. This balance is especially important with products with a short life cycle that can become obsolete. If not sold promptly, this might force you to deeply discount products to sell them. This dilemma can lead to incurring a loss.

Operations Management is the discipline focused on these issues and mitigating potential problems.

You can quickly assess how a company is doing by looking at its balance sheet, comparing Current Assets to Current Liabilities, and seeing if there is a larger amount of Current Assets. Make this comparison for the last few years, and you can see if there is a change in Working Capital and if it is due to a build-up of inventories.

FINDING FINANCIAL STATEMENTS TO ANALYZE

Now you know what information is conveyed in Financial Statements, how they are structured and presented, and techniques for analyzing them.

You can now use this knowledge to look up, review, and analyze companies. Look at other businesses in your line of work and compare how your company is doing in comparison to them. Or check out companies you might be interested in investing in. You can find tons of such information online related to publicly traded companies.

COMPANY-SPECIFIC FINANCIAL INFORMATION

Public companies are corporations that are traded on the stock market. Most large companies you are familiar with are publicly traded. Their stock price is listed in the paper, Yahoo! Finance, and other websites.

The Securities and Exchange Commission (SEC) regulates these companies and the stock markets. One of the requirements for these companies is to submit audited financial statements and descriptive information about their operations to the SEC. These annual reports, called **10Ks**, are available online for public review. You can now begin to put your newfound knowledge to use!

Look on the www.SEC.gov website for 10Ks of public companies. Besides their annual financial statements, public companies must also disclose information about their operations and strategies, such as:
  • Who they believe their competitors are,
  • How they plan to grow the business,
  • What does the general economy look like, and
  • How they predict it will affect their business segments.

. . .

These documents represent a wealth of expert opinion on your specific business domain and make for excellent and profitable reading.

———

COCA COLA PEPSI CO

FINANCIAL ANALYSIS

BALANCE SHEET

Balance sheet $ mio	Coca Cola	Pepsi	Difference
Cash	11,611	5,348	6,263
Account Receivable	3,487	10,163	6,676
Inventories	4,233	5,722	1,489
Other current assets	3,240	806	2,434
Current assets	22,581	21,539	1,052
Intangible assets	41,566	37,046	4,520
Tangible assets	9,841	24,291	14,450
Other investments and assets	18,755	9,311	9,454
Non-current assets	70,172	70,648	476
Total assets	92,763	92,187	576
Trade payables	15,865	20,852	4,987
Financial liabilities	2,772	3,141	369
Other liabilities	1,097	2,792	1,705
Current liabilities	19,734	26,785	7,061
Long term financial debt	36,377	35,657	720
Other long term liabilities	10,836	12,472	1,634
Long term fin. liabilities	47,213	48,129	916
Equity	25,826	17,273	8,553
Total Equity and liabilities	92,763	92,187	576

PROFITABILITY

Profitability ratios	Coca Cola	Pepsi	Diff
Gross profit margin	59.1%	53.9%	5%
EBITDA margin	35%	16%	18%
Net profit rate	24%	9%	15%
ROE	42%	48%	6%
ROCE	15%	13%	2%
ROA	12%	9%	3%
Revenue per employee	548	291	256
Profit per employee	131	26	104
EBITDA per employee	189	47	142
Free cash flow rate	23%	8%	15%

> Coca Cola is more profitable especially looking into net profitability which implies better expenditure utilization.

> Free cash flow rate is significantly better at Coca Cola that could be sign of better cash management.

LIQUIDITY

Liquidity	Coca Cola	Pepsi	Difference
Net working capital	(5,992)	(7,453)	1,461
Curr. assets - Curr. liabilities	2,847	(5,246)	8,113
Current ratio	1.15	0.80	0.3
Cash ratio	0.59	0.20	0.4
Quick ratio	0.77	0.58	0.2
Working capital ratio	3%	24%	27%

> Both companies recorded negative net working capital. They are significantly financed by account payables.

> Current ratio at Pepsi is less than 1 that is not good sign.

INCOME STATEMENT

	Coca Cola	Pepsi	Difference
Revenue	45,030	91,617	46,587
COGS	18,399	42,204	23,805
Gross profit	26,631	49,413	22,782
Overhead - variable	7,424	33,184	25,764
Overhead - fixed	5,149	0	5,149
Overhead costs	12,573	33,268	20,715
Other	(1,494)	1,423	2,917
EBITDA / Operating profit	15,552	14,702	(850)
Depreciation and amortisation	1,947	3,437	1,490
EBIT	13,605	11,265	(2,340)
Interest and financial expenses	1,418	875	(543)
Financial income	783		(783)
EBT	12,970	10,390	(2,580)
Tax	2,198	2,100	(98)
Net income	10,772	8,290	(2,482)

EFFICIENCY

Efficiency	Coca Cola	Pepsi	Diff
DSO	28	40	(12.2)
DIO	84	45	38.8
DPO	315	180	134.4
Cash conversion	(204)	(95)	(107.8)
Asset turnover	0.5	0.99	(0.5)
Fixed asset turnover	0.6	1.3	(0.7)
EBITDA TO interest	11	17	(5.9)
Opex per employee	152	106	46.7

> Pepsi is better is inventory efficiency

> Both companies have high DPO, either they have outstandingly good payment terms with suppliers or they have overdue payables. Should be checked.

STRUCTURE

Structure	Coca Cola	Pepsi	Diff.
Total COGS in Revenue	41%	46%	5%
COGS variable in revenue	41%	46%	5%
Overhead in revenue	28%	36%	8%
Interest expense in loans	3%	2%	1%
Equity ratio	28%	19%	9%
Debt ratio	72%	81%	9%
Fixed assets in total assets	76%	77%	1%

> Thanks to Goodwill, intangible assets shares almost 50% in total assets in both companies. This should be explored and tested on impairment.

QUESTIONS TO ASK

> What were changes in rations comparing last period

> What are variance from budget

> Is there a balance between profitability and liquidity?

> Why net working capital is negative?

> Why cash ratio is high?

> Is high ROE is sustainable?

> How has the operational efficiency changed over time?

> Why current ratio is less than 1

> Why revenue per employee is much lower than Coca Cola

> How has the operational efficiency changed over time?

> Why current ratio is less than 1

> Why revenue per employee is much lower than Coca Cola

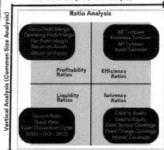

CHAPTER 9
HOW TO EVALUATE FINANCIAL STATEMENTS LIKE WARREN BUFFETT

VALUE INVESTING TENDS to be simplified to identifying numbers on a financial statement, comparing them with other companies, and evaluating how much one should pay for an investment.

A better explanation of value investing is understanding the cash movement in a company and understanding if managers are deploying capital effectively enough that the company makes a profit and maintains a competitive advantage.

Let's look at one of the ways Warren Buffett reads financial statements and footnotes to find winners. We'll do this with the help of a flow chart.

UNDERSTANDING PROFIT

Operating Profit is revenue minus operating expenses, where revenue is how the company makes money, and operating expense is what a company has spent in the reporting year. Profit, or Net Income, takes place before calculating and paying tax.

. . .

Dig into the footnotes accompanying the financial statements to find out about the operating segments, how revenue is made, and a breakdown of expenses.

Be wary of companies that don't provide meaningful segments (e.g., Lacking geographical segments) or do not even give a breakdown of expenses that satisfies your curiosity.

These are signs of companies that are obscuring their costs of doing business.

You can also calculate a company's operating profit margin by dividing operating Profit by revenue. This calculation is one of Warren Buffet's preferred financial ratios.

Operating Profit Margin = Operating Profit/Revenue.

Using the operating profit margin, you can compare a company's performance to others in the same industry.

What management does with owned earnings matters.

Retained earnings are the net Profit a business retains after dividends are paid out.

. . .

The importance of retained earnings is how a company uses them. Some common ones include buyback of shares, investments, payments for property, plant, and equipment, or repaying debt.

Make sure retained earnings are going to good use.

Buffett's rule of thumb is to calculate ten years' worth of retained earnings and compare it to a company's growth in market value for the same time range. So, he's expecting more than one dollar in market value to be created for every dollar retained.

PAY ATTENTION TO PROPERTY, PLANT, AND EQUIPMENT.

Property, plant, and equipment (PPE) are the income-producing and cost-saving assets that keep a company running. The importance of these items is how a company has allocated its capital to create value.

Assets lose their Balance Sheet value over time through depreciation and amortization.

Because of depreciation and amortization, Warren Buffett looks for companies that roughly match their 5-year average capital expenditures (CAPEX) to their yearly depreciation and amortization.
    Depreciation expense is in the Income Statement. Capital expenditures (CAPEX) show up in the investment section of the Cash Flow Statement as payments for property, plant, and equipment.

Compare depreciation and amortization to payments for property, plant, and equipment and make sure they are reasonably close.

. . .

For example:

Check out Apple 2022 Cash Flow Statement: Warren Buffett approves of the CAPEX charges relative to the Depreciation and Amortization expenses.

Conclusion

Understand how the three financial statements are interconnected and how cash flows within a company, and you'll be an expert investor and a profitable businessperson.

———

Warren Buffet's Financial Statement Investment Criteria

	METRIC	EQUATION	THRESHOLD
INCOME STATEMENT	Gross Margin	$\dfrac{\text{Gross Profit}}{\text{Revenue}}$	>40%
	SG&A Margin	$\dfrac{\text{SG\&A}}{\text{Gross Profit}}$	<30%
	R&D Margin	$\dfrac{\text{R\&D}}{\text{Gross Profit}}$	<30%
	Depreciation Margin	$\dfrac{\text{Depreciation}}{\text{Gross Profit}}$	<10%
	Interest Margin	$\dfrac{\text{Interest Expense}}{\text{Operating Income}}$	<15%
	Tax Margin	$\dfrac{\text{Taxes}}{\text{Pre-Tax Income}}$	Corporate Tax Rate
	Net Income Margin	$\dfrac{\text{Net Income}}{\text{Revenue}}$	>20%
	EPS Growth	$\dfrac{\text{Year 2 EPS}}{\text{Year 1 EPS}}$	Positive & Growing
BALANCE SHEET	Cash & Debt	Cash > Debt	Cash > Debt
	Adjusted Debt to Equity	$\dfrac{\text{Total Liabilities}}{\text{Shareholder Equity + Treasury Stock}}$	Below 0.80
	Preferred Stock	NONE	NONE
	Retained Earnings	$\dfrac{\text{Year 2 Retained Earnings}}{\text{Year 1 Retained Earnings}}$	Consistent Growth
	Treasury Stock	Treasury Stock > 1	Exists
CASH FLOW STATEMENT	Capex Margin	$\dfrac{\text{Capex}}{\text{Net income}}$	<25%

WORKING CAPITAL VS INVESTED CAPITAL

Operational orientation / short term

Strategic orientation / long term

DEFINITION

The difference between a company's current assets (short-term resources) and current liabilities (short-term obligations). It measures a company's liquidity and ability to meet its day-to-day operational needs. Provides a buffer against unexpected cash flow disruptions. involves optimizing current assets and liabilities to improve liquidity

The total amount of money invested in a company or project. This can include equity from shareholders, debt from lenders, and retained earnings. It represents the total capital employed for generating returns . Provides a buffer against unexpected cash flow disruptions. used in metrics like return on invested capital (ROIC) to evaluate profitability and efficiency.

CALCULATION

1. Working Capital = Current Assets – Current Liabilities

2. Working Capital = Current Assets (less cash) – Current Liabilities (less debt)

3. (Net) WC = Accounts Receivable (AR) + Inventory (I) – Accounts Payable (AP)

1. Operational approach : Net Working Capital + PPE + Goodwill + Intangibles

2. Financing approach: Total debt and leases + Total equity and equity equivalents

FORECASTING

1. Make best estimate of Revenues and COGS
2. Based on historical data on AP, I and AR balance, calculate historical DSO, DIO and DPO.
3. Make best estimate of these indicators as assumptions for forecast relevant WC categories.
4. Or simply build 3 statement model and calculate WC

1. Project future equity (including retained earnings) and debt levels based on strategic plans and financing decisions.
2. Use current debt schedule & make planed debt schedules to make full debt forecast debt. Make CAPEX and NWC schedules.
3. Or simply build 3 statement model and calculate IC

RATIOS

Working capital Turnover
Working capital / Average assets
Measures the relationship between a company's net working capital and its total assets.

WC share in sales
Working capital / Sales
Measures how efficiently a company uses its working capital to generate sales

Return on invested capital (ROIC)
ROIC = EBIT x (1- tax) / Invested capital
Gives insight into how effectively a company is using the money invested in it to generate profits. It's a metric that can help investors determine the quality of a management and their ability to generate a return on the total capital

HOW TO IMPROVE

1. Improve inventory turnover to reduce excess stock.
2. Implement efficient collection strategies and possibly renegotiate payment terms with customers.
3. Optimize payment terms with suppliers without damaging relationships.

1. Optimize Capital Structure: Find the right balance between debt and equity to minimize the cost of capital and maximize value.
2. Investment Decisions: Make strategic decisions about where to invest capital for the best returns.

CHAPTER 10
WHY IT'S IMPORTANT TO READ ANNUAL REPORTS EVEN IF YOU CAN'T AFFORD TO INVEST

IT'S MORE than just information on which you base your investment choices.

A general assumption is that you should only read annual reports when you have money to invest.

Why else would I read a boring 100 to 200-page document?

Suppose you are at that stage where you should find potential investments to make it big, like side hustles and entrepreneurship. Saving and investing may be different from your priorities. However, you might keep looking for the 'just-in-case' moment.

I gave it some thought.
    Are there any reasons to keep reading annual reports even though you currently have no money to invest?

. . .

The initial answer was no.

Why bother?

The time spent reading could be better spent elsewhere — spending time with the family or taking up a new hobby.

I let this thought ruminate until I realized this was a false choice because I'd be losing a skill I had taken years to build. Secondly, the annual report contains more knowledge than an opinion blog piece from The Motley Fool or The Wall Street Journal.

I'll explain why you should continue reading an annual report regardless of whether you have money to invest because you might be surprised by what further benefits these lengthy documents can bring.

1. IT'S A DISCLOSURE DOCUMENT THAT YOU CAN EXPLOIT TO BEAT YOUR COMPETITORS.

The annual report is a public disclosure document made mandatory for publication after the 1929 stock market crash.

The annual report contains all the information you can learn about a company that isn't confidential. It's far more thorough than the blog posts and puff pieces you see on a company's website investor relations section.

So, why would you want to read everything about a company if you won't invest money in it?

Here's a pretty simple reason:

If you're job hunting, you can easily beat the competition by knowing more about the company than others competing for the same role.

Bosses are impressed if you can list a company's strategic goals and how your skills complement such goals.

For example, I once went to a data analyst interview whose purpose was to clean data.

This opportunity wasn't a formidable job, and the pay was decent, so I knew the competition would be fierce.

Why not read the company's annual report and list some of its strategic goals at the interview to differentiate me?

The preparation paid off. At the interview was one of those 'high-ranking company leaders' who was there at the interview to meet quota.

The interview went well because I managed to impress the highest-paid person there, who also had the least technical experience among the interviewers, by listing company goals.

She seemed particularly thrilled that I was more than just a nerd. I was a nerd who understood business talk.

And yes, I did get an offer for the job.

Takeaway: Just by being able to recite critical points from the annual report, you'll sound impressive in interviews.

2. IT HELPS YOU RETAIN YOUR ACCOUNTING KNOWLEDGE.

The owners of Berkshire Hathaway give two sound pieces of advice.

Warren Buffett: Accounting is the language of business.

Charlie Munger: Use it or lose it.

What do both snippets of wisdom together mean?

If you want to maintain your skills in reading financial statements, you must read them often.

Unless you're an accountant or a manager of finances, where can you get financial information to practice your skills?

The best place is the 10K annual reports.

For instance, I began learning accounting to find valuable companies to invest in.

Accounting was a challenge to learn. I enjoyed it a little, but I got better at it after much persistence.

However, ever since finding what I wanted to invest in, I got a bit lazy and wasn't interested in reading annual reports anymore.

This attitude was a mistake.

When I wanted to read up on the finances of a particular company that sparked my interest, my abilities had atrophied.

I forgot what some of the numbers meant. Sure, I looked up the meaning, but my skills were slower than they used to be.

I had to relearn accounting again. Yes, learning was a bit faster, but still a pain studying it again.

Takeaway: To keep your annual report skills agile and fresh, you still need to keep reading them regardless of whether you're putting money into the market.

Use it or lose it.

3. IT EXPANDS YOUR GENERAL KNOWLEDGE OF THE BUSINESS WORLD.

Warren Buffett says he gets most of his information from annual reports.

It's not from analyst summaries or industry reports but from annual reports.

I still needed to figure out why until I began reading annual reports extensively myself.

If you read annual reports from the first page to the last page, you will know everything about the company and the industry it operates in.

For instance, before I read Walgreens's annual report, I only knew a little about it other than it was a big pharmacy chain in the US.

However, after reading its annual report, I soon discovered that Walgreens is Walgreens Boots Alliance, where Boots is a UK-based pharmacy chain. The company is also a holding company, which means that it is the parent company that doesn't run each pharmacy but instead holds an interest in them.

Yes, you can find information on its Wikipedia page, but it's only via the annual report that you can understand how a company operates with its business model.

Furthermore, I was surprised to learn that Walgreens operates as a low-margin business that uses its volume (a Walgreens pharmacy located within 5 miles of 78% of Americans) to make the bulk of its earnings. Furthermore, its size also gives it purchasing power when dealing with suppliers.

Ultimately, this isn't a business I want to enter (I'm not a fan of low-margin companies). Still, Walgreens' annual report helped me understand more precisely what makes a successful pharmacy chain versus an unprofitable one.

Takeaway: If you want to understand how businesses work, you need to read the annual report. Doing this puts the financial numbers into context and helps you understand the business world better.

4. IT IMPROVES YOUR DECISION-MAKING PROCESS.

The most important reason to maintain your annual report reading skills is so that you can evaluate your forecasts in the following year or two.

You'll only know if you're a good predictor of companies once you get feedback. Unfortunately, this can take months or years.

I remember reading about a particular company with decent company finances. I considered buying it, except it relied heavily on exports, and with lockdowns and heavy tariffs against its products due to political reasons, I gave it a pass.

Fast forward a year later, and with trade happening again, the company's stock price jumped up by 50%.

Maybe the finances deteriorated slightly from increased borrowings, but the market thought otherwise.

Upon reflection, I ignored how strong the company's branding was and that not even tariffs could reduce its demand.

Yes, I missed out on some easy returns, so reading its annual report helped confirm the company was decent.

Takeaway: Even if you don't put money into the market, at least by regularly reading annual reports, regardless of whether you are investing, you'll have a feedback loop on your predictions.

Conclusions: Yes, you should still read annual reports even when you are not actively looking to invest.

Keeping up reading annual reports is good not just for your investing skills but also for your career and intellectual skills. Of course, you could ignore the writing and read the financial statements, but you'll rob yourself of knowledge and wisdom.

. . .

Here's a summary of the key takeaways:

• Reading annual reports gives you a vital understanding of the company's strategic goals, operations, and company issues. You can capitalize on them at interviews and in your resumes.

• Continuing to read them, regardless of the motivation of the business cycle, will give you a competitive knowledge advantage when the market is ripe for buying.

• Reading annual reports gives you a broad understanding of all the businesses and industries in your circle of competence. This broad understanding increases your chances of making a good investment.

• Being a good investor is all about the process. You can only improve by getting feedback. Reading annual reports early and getting feedback later is the best way to improve your investing skills without putting any money in.

———

Investing Ratios

RATIO	FORMULA	MEASSURE OF
LIQUIDITY AND EFFICIENCY		
QUICK RATIO	$\dfrac{\text{Cash \& Equivalents + Receivables}}{\text{Current Liabilities}}$	Immediate short-term debt-paying ability
CURRENT RATIO	$\dfrac{\text{Current Assets}}{\text{Current Liabilities}}$	Short-term debt-paying ability
ACCOUNTS RECEIVABLE TURNOVER	$\dfrac{\text{Net Sales}}{\text{Average Accounts Receivables}}$	Efficiency of collection
INVENTORY TURNOVER	$\dfrac{\text{Cost of Good Sold}}{\text{Average Inventory}}$	Efficiency of Inventory management
DAYS' SALES UNCOLLECTED	$\dfrac{\text{Accounts Receivable}}{\text{Net Sales}} \times 365$	Liquidity of receivables
DAYS' SALES IN INVENTORY	$\dfrac{\text{Ending Inventory}}{\text{Cost of Good Sold}} \times 365$	Liquidity of inventory
TOTAL ASSET TURNOVER	$\dfrac{\text{Net Sales}}{\text{Average Total Assets}}$	Efficiency of assets in producing sales
SOLVENCY		
DEBT RATIO	$\dfrac{\text{Total liabilities}}{\text{Total assets}}$	Creditor financing and leverage
EQUITY RATIO	$\dfrac{\text{Total equity}}{\text{Total assets}}$	Owner financing
DEBT-TO-EQUITY RATIO	$\dfrac{\text{Total liabilities}}{\text{Total equity}}$	Debt versus equity financing
TIMES INTEREST EARNED	$\dfrac{\text{Earnings Before Interest \& Taxes}}{\text{Interest Expense}}$	Protection in meeting interest payments
PROFITABILITY		
GROSS MARGIN	$\dfrac{\text{Revenue - Cost of Good Sold}}{\text{Revenue}}$	Gross Profit in each sales dollar
PROFIT MARGIN	$\dfrac{\text{Earnings}}{\text{Net Sales}}$	Net income In each sales dollar
RETURN ON ASSETS	$\dfrac{\text{Net Income}}{\text{Average Total Assets}}$	Overall profitability of assets
RETURN ON EQUITY	$\dfrac{\text{Net Income - Preferred Dividends}}{\text{Average Common Stockholders' Equity}}$	Profitability of owner investment
BOOK VALUE PER SHARE	$\dfrac{\text{Shareholders' Equity}}{\text{Shares Outstanding}}$	Liquidation at reported amounts
EARNINGS PER SHARE	$\dfrac{\text{Net Income - Preferred Dividends}}{\text{Shares Outstanding}}$	Net income per share
MARKET PROSPECTS		
PRICE TO EARNINGS RATIO	$\dfrac{\text{Share Price}}{\text{Earnings Per Share}}$	Market value relative to earnings
DIVIDEND YIELD	$\dfrac{\text{Annual Cash Dividends per Share}}{\text{Share Price}}$	Cash return per share owned

CHAPTER 11
USERS OF ACCOUNTING INFORMATION

USERS OF ACCOUNTING INFORMATION

MANAGEMENT NEEDS to know how the overall company is performing or how their division is doing. Managers may need feedback ASAP on how a new marketing campaign or pricing strategy is working. When and how transactions are booked is very important to users of accounting information. Users need timely information about how the business is doing in order to make decisions.

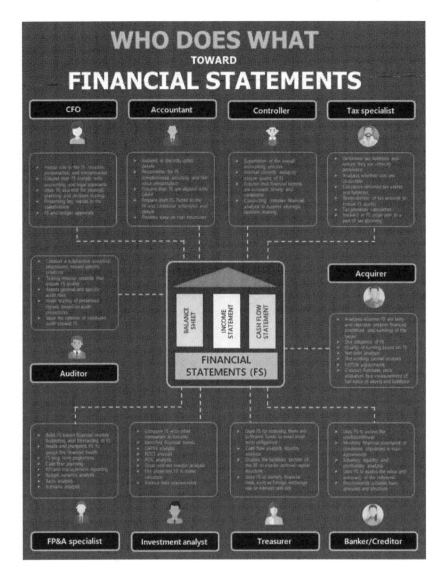

Besides the internal interests of management, there are external users of accounting information such as:

- Bankers who are interested in your credit worthiness and ability to repay loans,
- Vendors who are interested in your ability to pay and your credit worthiness,

- Investors who want to know whether to invest or how their investment is performing,
- Stock Analysts who research companies and opine on whether or not they are good investments for their clients,
- Potential customers, especially of big ticket items or services, who want to know that the company is sound and will be around to offer support and spare parts, and
- Taxing authorities who want to know how much money the business has made or lost.

Reporting the results of business activity on an accrual basis is important to these parties that have a stake in the company's performance and health. Accrual provides a much more accurate picture of the operations to those who are not intimately involved in the day-to-day operations but need to know the operational details.

The way this kind of reporting of the accounting information is prepared, organized, and conveyed is in Financial Statements.

WHO USES FINANCIAL STATEMENTS?

→ MBA ASAP ←

USERS	PURPOSE OF USE	CONCERN AREAS
Shareholders/ Investors	To assess the performance of the company and make decisions regarding buying, holding, or selling shares.	➡ Earnings per share (EPS) ➡ Dividend payment history ➡ Return on equity (ROE) ➡ Growth trends and potential
Analysts	To provide recommendations or insights to investors and other stakeholders about the company's financial performance.	➡ Underlying trends in financial statements ➡ Projections and future estimates ➡ Comparative analysis with industry peers
Creditors/Lenders	To evaluate the creditworthiness of the company and its ability to repay loans or provide ongoing credit.	➡ Liquidity ratios (e.g., current ratio) ➡ Solvency ratios (e.g., debt-to-equity ratio) ➡ Cash flow from operating activities
Employees & Labor	To understand the company's profitability and stability, which can affect job security, wages, and benefits.	➡ Profitability trends ➡ Company's expansion and hiring plans ➡ Employee benefits and compensation disclosures
Management	To make informed decisions about the company's operations, strategy, and future direction.	➡ Segment-wise profitability ➡ Key performance indicators ➡ Budget vs actual performance
Regulators & Government	To ensure compliance with financial reporting standards and tax obligations.	➡ Tax liabilities and payments ➡ Compliance with financial regulations ➡ Any contingent liabilities or off-balance-sheet financing
Competitors	To benchmark and compare their own performance and strategy against the company.	➡ Profit margins ➡ Market share data ➡ Strategic initiatives disclosed

CHAPTER 12
FINANCIAL STATEMENTS GLOSSARY OF TERMS

THESE ARE important words and phrases, in alphabetical order, related to Reading and Understanding Financial Statements:

ACCOUNTING

Accounting is the recording and reporting of financial transactions of an enterprise. It includes the recording the origination of the transaction like a sale or the receipt of a bill in the mail, its recognition in the ledger books, its processing for payment or deposit in the bank, and the summarization and presentation in the financial statements. This quantitative financial information is critical to running a company, paying taxes, and making operating and investment decisions.

ACCOUNTS PAYABLE

Accounts Payable is a liability representing an amount owed to a creditor. In most companies checks are cut in batches and obligations are first entered through Accounts Payable accounts before they are paid. It is normally a current liability showing on the Balance Sheet. Accounts Payable is an amount owed *by* the enterprise for delivered goods or services provided. Accounts Payable is an account associated with the Accrual method of accounting.

ACCOUNTS RECEIVABLE

Account Receivable is an amount owed *to* the enterprise from a completed sales transaction or for services rendered. Accounts Receivable is an asset related to sales revenue. Accounts Receivable is a current asset. Accounts Receivalbe is an account associated with the Accrual method of accounting.

ACCRUAL BASIS

Accrual basis is a method of accounting that recognizes revenue when earned, rather than when money is actually collected and expenses when incurred rather than when paid. It is the method of recognizing revenues as goods are sold, or delivered, and when services are rendered. This recognition of a transaction occurring is independent of the time when cash is received.

Expenses are recognized in the period when the related revenue is recognized. Accrual basis creates an accurate picture of transactions and makes sure the revenue generated and the expenses associated with that revenue are recognized and booked at the same time. Enterprises use the accrual basis for their accounting as opposed to a cash basis. Accrual accounting is a consequence of implementing the **Matching Principle**.

ADDITIONAL PAID-IN CAPITAL (APIC)

The Additional Paid-in Capital (APIC) account is where the amount paid for a share of stock, less the par value, is recorded. It is an Equity Account that shows up on the Balance Sheet. Another alternative title for the account is *capital contributed in excess of par value*.

AMORTIZATION

Amortization is the process of liquidating or extinguishing a debt with a series of payments that include both principal and interest, to the creditor. It refers to the calculation and payment schedule of the paying off of debt with fixed repayments in regular installments over a period of time. Consumers are most likely to encounter amortization with a mortgage or car loan. Amortization can mean the accounting for the payments themselves.

Amortization can also mean the spreading out of capital expenses for intangible assets, such as a patent or trademark, over a specific period of time. This time is usually over the asset's estimated useful life for accounting and tax purposes. Amortization is similar to depreciation, which is used for tangible assets, and to depletion, which is used with natural resources. The intent of Amortization is to match an asset's expense with the revenue it generates.

AMORTIZATION SCHEDULE

An amortization schedule for a mortgage is a table showing the allocation between interest and principle of each payment. Each payment has a different mix of interest and principal. As the payments progress through the schedule the amount of interest decreases and the principal increases as a fraction of the total payment. The total payment is the same each period.

ASSET

Assets are what an enterprise owns. An asset is defined as having probable future economic benefits obtained or controlled by an entity as a result of past transactions. Examples of assets are: land, factories, office buildings, equipment, vehicles, cash in bank accounts, other investments, accounts receivable, and intellectual property such as patents and trademarks.

Assets are purchased and funded by two classes of obligations that the enterprise incurs: Liabilities and Equity. Liabilities and Equity can be thought of as the sources of funding to purchases and retain Assets.

BALANCE SHEET

A Balance Sheet is a summary report of a company's financial position on a specific date that shows Total Assets = Total Liabilities + Owner's Equity. The Balance Sheet is one of the two most basic financial statements, the other being the Income Statement.

Think of a Balance Sheet in terms of your home ownership which has the three components of Asset, Liability and Equity. The Asset is the value of the house. This is determined by an appraisal. An appraisal takes into account recent sales of homes in the area and compensates for differences like the number of bath or bedrooms, the size of the lot, etc. The Liability is the mortgage. This is how much you owe against the house. The Equity is the difference between the Value of the Asset and the amount of the Liability. If your home is worth $200,000 and you have a remaining mortgage balance of $150,000, then you have $50,000 in Equity. We sometimes call this homeowner's equity.

If your mortgage balance is more than the value of the home, then you are considered "upside down" or "under water". The same principle applies to a business: if the value of its Liabilities is more than the value of the Assets then the enterprise is insolvent and probably headed for bankruptcy.

THE BOOKS

The "books" is a slang general accounting term referring to the General Ledger and the various journals that are kept by a business. *Book* can be used as a verb meaning to record a transaction.

BOOK VALUE

Book value is the value of an asset according to its balance sheet account balance. For assets, the value is based on the original cost of the asset less any depreciation, amortization or impairment costs made against the asset. Book value refers to the net amount.

Book value can differ from Market value if the asset has gained value while it has been owned or lost significant value. An example would be an office building owned by a company that has increased in value but is carried on the books at cost minus depreciation. Assets like stocks and bonds most likely have a different current market value than what they were purchased for.

CAPITALIZE

To capitalize is to record an expenditure on an asset that will benefit future periods rather than to treat the entire amount as an expense in the period of its occurrence. It is an accounting method used to delay the recognition of a significant expense by recording the expense as a long-term asset. Capitalizing significant expenses more accurately depicts the situation. If a company buys a new machine that will be productive for ten years then one tenth of the expense should be taken in each year of its operation. Companies acquiring new assets with a long-term lifespan can spread out the cost over a specified period of time. That period of time is an estimate of the asset's useful life, when it will be contributing to the generation of revenues.

CASH

Cash is currency and coins, negotiable checks, and balances in bank accounts. We all know what cash is but in accounting it refers to the first account in the Assets category of the Balance Sheet. This is aggregated from all company bank accounts and it is derived as the bottom number on the Cash Flow Statement. The cash amount at the bottom of the Cash Flow Statement must reconcile with the total amount of all bank account balances.

CASH FLOW STATEMENT

The cash flow statement is a financial statement that shows how changes in balance sheet accounts and income statement affect cash. The cash flow statement breaks the analysis down into three sections: operating, investing and financing activities.

COMMON STOCK

Common Stock is the type of stock present in every corporation. Shares of common stock provide evidence of ownership in a corporation. These shares represent the class of owners who have residual claims on the assets and earnings of a corporation after all debt and preferred shareholders' claims have been met.

Holders of common stock elect the corporation's directors at the annual meeting. Common stock receives the distribution of profits of the company via dividends. If the corporation were to liquidate, the secured lenders would be paid first, followed by unsecured lenders, preferred stockholders, and lastly the common stockholders. If a company is acquired, the proceeds go to the shareholders after the debts are paid off.

COST OF GOODS SOLD

Cost of Goods Sold (COGS) is the direct costs attributable to the production of the goods sold by a company. This amount includes the cost of the materials used in creating the good along with the direct labor costs used to produce the good. It *excludes* indirect expenses such as distribution costs, marketing and sales force costs. Measuring COGS is at the core of Cost Accounting which is considered its own sub discipline within accounting.

CURRENT ASSETS

Current Assets are balance sheet accounts that represent the value of assets that are reasonably expected to be converted into cash within one year. Current assets include cash, accounts receivable, inventory, marketable securities, prepaid expenses and other liquid assets that can be readily converted to cash. Current Assets are related to measuring the liquidity of an enterprise: how quickly a company can convert assets to cash to cover expenses and weather a crisis.

DEBT

Debt is an amount owed for funds borrowed. Debt is the general name and category for loans, notes, bonds, mortgages, debentures and the like that are evidence of amounts owed and have definite payment dates and schedules. The lender agrees to lend funds to the borrower upon a promise by the borrower to pay interest on the debt, usually with the interest to be paid at regular intervals. Debt is a Liability to the company (an asset to the lender) and is shown on the balance sheet net of how much has been repaid.

There are many varieties and "tiers" of debt based on repayment schedules and conditions and on the seniority of the claims on assets. In case of bankruptcy the most senior debt gets paid first from the liquidation of assets and the more junior note holder get paid next. The more junior the debt, the higher the risk of getting repaid and so the higher the interest rate that investors require. There is senior debt, junior debt, mezzanine debt, and convertible debt. Convertible debt has the option to convert into common stock.

DEPRECIATION

Depreciation is the method used to allocate the cost of a tangible asset over its useful life. It is the process of apportioning the purchase price of an asset to the periods in which the benefits of using it occur. This provides a more accurate picture of assigning costs to the revenues they help produce.

Businesses depreciate long-term assets for both tax and accounting purposes. Accelerating depreciation can provide a larger expense in early periods and this can shelter income from taxes. Different depreciation schedules are used for different fixed assets. Depreciation schedules can vary in length and also in how fast depreciation is incurred. There are accelerated depreciation techniques that apply more depreciation to early years in the schedule.

Depreciation is also used to describe a decrease in an asset's value caused by unfavorable market conditions.

DIVIDEND

A dividend is a payment made by a corporation to its shareholders, usually as a distribution of a portion of profits. When a corporation earns a profit or surplus, it can re-invest it in the business; this is called retained earnings, and/or pay out some of the profit as a dividend to shareholders. A dividend can be paid in cash (a cash dividend) or stock (a stock dividend).

EQUITY

Equity is what the shareholders or owner of a company actually own. It is a claim on assets. Equity is short for owner's equity or shareholder's equity. It consists of the net value, net of liabilities, of the assets of an enterprise. It is the residual interest in the assets of an entity that remains after deducting its liabilities. Net assets are the difference between the total assets of the entity and all its liabilities. Equity appears on the balance sheet below Liabilities. Remember the balance sheet formula: Assets = Liabilities + Equity.

Think of this concept in terms of your home: the appraised value of the home is the Asset, the mortgage is the Liability, and the difference between the two is the Equity. This is the same relationship between the three entities on a corporate balance sheet.

EXPENSE

An expense is the term used for funds paid by the enterprise. For example: paychecks to employees, and payments to vendors for goods or services, rent, the electric bill, supplies, you get the idea.

Another way to think of expenses is as a decrease in owners' equity caused by the using up, or depletion, of assets in producing revenue or carrying out other activities that are part of the company's operations.

FASB

FASB stands for Financial Accounting Standards Board and is an independent, private, nongovernmental authority for the establishment of *generally accepted accounting principles,* generally referred to as GAAP, in the United States.

Financial Statements, and the accounting practices that produce them, must adhere to these rules and principles to be considered accurate, truthful and transparent.

FINANCIAL STATEMENTS

Financial Statements are a group of reports showing a summary view of the financial activities and status of a company. There are three major financial statements: Balance Sheet, Income Statement, and Cash Flow Statement. Each statement tells a different story about the financial activity of an enterprise. Financial statements also include the notes provided to explain and give more insight into the numbers.

FISCAL YEAR

A fiscal year is a period of 12 consecutive months chosen by a business as its accounting period for annual reporting purposes. Most fiscal years are a calendar year (January 1- December 31) but a fiscal year can start and end on any month. For example most U.S. government agencies run a fiscal year from October 1 – September 30.

FIXED ASSET

A fixed asset is any tangible item with a useful life of more than one year. Fixed Assets include office buildings, factories, major equipment and vehicles. Computers used to be thought of as fixed assets but personal computers now cost less than $1,000 and have useful lives of not much more than a year because of the accelerated rate of technical innovation. So now, most computers are usually expensed instead of capitalized as a fixed asset. A fixed asset is a long term asset and is listed on the Balance Sheet after the current assets.

GAAP

GAAP stands for Generally Accepted Accounting Principles which are conventions, rules, and procedures that are required to be followed in preparing financial statements. GAAP defines accepted accounting practice in the United States. These principles are defined and overseen by FASB. They include both broad guidelines and detailed practices and procedures.

INCOME STATEMENT

An Income Statement is a summary report that shows revenues, expenses, gains or losses over a specific period of time, typically a month, quarter or fiscal year. An income statement is structured as: Revenue – Expenses = Net Income. Net Income is also referred to as Profit or Earnings.

The *earnings-per-share* amount is usually also shown on the income statement. This is calculated by dividing the Earnings by the number of share of stock outstanding.

INTELLECTUAL PROPERTY

Intellectual Property (IP) is the asset category that describes and details the set of intangible assets owned by a company. These IP assets are legally protected from outside use or implementation without consent. From an accounting standpoint, Intellectual property can consist of patents, copyrights, and trademarks. Intellectual Property assets are listed on the balance sheet and valued at the cost of procuring them net of amortization.

LEVERAGE

Leverage is the business term for the dynamic difference between two categories. The two main uses of the term are in association with operations and finance.

Operating leverage refers to the tendency of net income to rise at a faster rate than sales when there are fixed costs.

Financial leverage means the use of long-term debt in securing funds for the enterprise. A measure of financial leverage is the debt to equity ratio. It is calculated as the ratio of a company's loan capital (debt) to the value of its common stock (equity) or Debt/Equity. Financial leverage adds risk to a company as debt repayments are consistent and revenues or sales may vary and not be enough to cover debt payments.

LIABILITY

A liability is an obligation to pay a definite amount at a definite time in return for a past or current benefit. It is what the company owes. For example: loans, taxes, payables, long term debt from a bond issue.

Liabilities on the Balance Sheet are categorized as Current, to be paid within the fiscal year, or Long Term, to be paid at a time further in the future.

LINE OF CREDIT

A line of credit is an arrangement between a financial institution, usually a bank, and a customer for short term borrowings on demand. The borrower can draw down on the line of credit at any time, but cannot exceed the maximum set in the agreement. A line of credit is similar to a personal credit card. It is used by a company to smooth out the need for operating funds to pay bills and other obligations when current assets like accounts receivable or inventory are slow in turning into cash.

LIQUIDITY

Liquidity refers to the availability of cash, or near cash resources like marketable securities, for meeting a firm's obligations. A measure of liquidity, or the ability of current assets to meet the obligations of current liabilities, is the current ratio. The current ratio is calculated as current assets/current liabilities. The current assets include inventory which is not so easy to convert quickly into cash.

The quick ratio is another measure that matches the most easily liquidated portions of current assets with current liabilities. It is used to evaluate whether a business has sufficient assets that can be converted into cash to pay its bills. The current assets that are included in the quick ratio are cash, marketable securities, and accounts receivable. Inventory is not included in the ratio, since it can be difficult to sell off quickly with incurring a significant loss. The quick ratio is a better indicator than the current ratio of the ability of a company to pay its immediate obligations because it excludes inventory from the calculation.

MARK-TO-MARKET

Mark-to-market is the term used for fair value accounting. It refers to accounting for the "fair value" of an asset or liability based on its current market price or some other objectively assessed value. Fair value accounting has been a part of Generally Accepted Accounting Principles (GAAP) in the United States since the early 1990s.

NET INCOME (LOSS)

Net Income (or loss) is the amount the company made or lost for a specific period of time. It is the excess of all revenues and gains for a period over all expenses and losses of the period. It is the bottom number on the Income Statement, and the top number on the Cash Flow Statement. To arrive at net income take total revenues minus total expenses. Net Income is also called Profit or Earnings.

P & L RESPONSIBILITY

P&L stands for profit and loss statement or income statement. P & L responsibility is one of the most important responsibilities of any executive position. It involves monitoring, and being judged on, the net income after expenses for a department or entire organization. The executive's performance is judged on the financial results. The executive has direct influence on how company resources are allocated and how tactics are developed to implement strategy.

Internal financial statements must be generated in order to evaluate an executive's performance who has P&L responsibility.

PAR VALUE

Par value is the face amount of a security. The Par Value account is a stock equity account shown on the Balance Sheet. Stock par value is used to keep track of the amount of shares outstanding. The par value is a small monetary value attributed to each share. It is an arbitrary number, usually $.01

Par value is also a term used for the face value of bonds. Most bonds sell at an initial, or par value, of $1,000. As interests change over the term of the bond, its value is either calculated as a premium of discount, from par value. This is how bonds can trade at yields that vary from the fixed interest rate at issuance.

PREFERRED STOCK

Preferred Stock is a class of stock with claims to income or assets after bondholders but before common shareholders. Preferred stock also provides for preferential treatment of dividends. Preferred stockholders will be paid dividends before the common stockholders receive dividends. These dividends are sometimes paid in stock instead of cash. Some preferred stock also has the ability to be converted into common stock.

PRINCIPAL

Principal refers to the face amount of a loan. It is the original sum invested or lent. In most bonds the principal is held and paid back in full at the end of the term of the bond. In amortized loans, like a mortgage, interest and principal are paid back as part of each payment. This schedule of payments and the fraction that is interest and principal is called an amortization table.

RETAINED EARNINGS

Retained earnings is the percentage of net income not paid out as dividends, but *retained* by the company to be reinvested in its core business, or to pay down debt. It is recorded under shareholders' equity on the balance sheet and is measured as owners' equity less contributed capital.

REVENUE

Revenue is funds collected by the company usually from sales. It is the monetary measure of sales or services rendered. Revenue is the top line on the Income Statement.

SEC

Securities and Exchange Commission, the agency authorized by the U.S. Congress to regulate financial markets and, among other things, the financial reporting practices of publicly traded corporations. Their website is www.sec.gov

SHARES OUTSTANDING

Shares outstanding is the amount of a company's stock currently held by all its shareholders, including restricted shares owned by the company's officers and insiders. Outstanding shares are shown on a company's balance sheet under the heading "Capital Stock." The number of outstanding shares is used in calculating key metrics such as a company's market capitalization (the stock price * shares outstanding), as well as its earnings per share (Earnings/shares outstanding).

STOCK

Stock, or shares, is the general term used to describe the ownership certificates of a company. Stocks are the investment instrument or vehicle of equity. Each share of stock represents a fractional ownership in the company.

CHAPTER 13
Q&A

THESE ARE questions and answers that I initially published on Quora related to Accounting, Financial Statements, Financial Analysis, and Corporate Finance.

ACCOUNTING

WHAT IS THE DIFFERENCE BETWEEN REVENUE AND EBITDA?

Both are Income Statement numbers. Revenue is the top line on the Income Statement. It is the money from sales. EBITDA is what is left from Revenue after expenses have been subtracted. EBITDA stands for Earnings Before Interest Taxes Depreciation and Amortization.

Earnings, Profit, and Net Income are all terms for the same number. They are synonyms.

Here is more information on the Income Statement and how to read one.

INCOME STATEMENT

The Income Statement can be summarized as: Revenues less Expenses equals Net Income. The term Net Income simply means Income (Revenues) *net* (less) of Expenses. Net Income is also called Profit or Earnings. Revenues are sometimes called Sales.

You understand this concept intuitively. We always strive to sell things for more than they cost us to make. When you buy a house you hope that it will appreciate in value so you can sell it in the future for more than you paid for it. In order to have a sustainable business model in the long run, the same logic applies. You can't sell things for less than they cost you to make and stay in business for long.

Think of the Income Statement in relation to your monthly personal finances. You have your monthly revenues: in most cases a salary from your job. You apply that monthly income to your monthly expenses: rent or mortgage, car loan, food, gas, utilities, clothes, phone, entertainment, etc. Our goal is to have our expenses be less than our income.

Over time, and with experience, we become better managers of our personal finances and begin to realize that we shouldn't spend more that we make. We strive to have some money left over at the end of the month that we can set aside and save. What we set aside and save is called **Retained Earnings**.

Some of what we set aside we may **invest** with an eye toward future benefits. We may invest in stocks and bonds or mutual funds, or we may invest in education to expand our future earning and working prospects. This is the same type of money management discipline that is applied in business. It's just a matter of scale. There are a few additional zeros after the numbers on a large company's Income Statement but the idea is the same.

This concept applies to all businesses. **Revenues** are usually from Sales of products or services. **Expenses** are what you spend to support the operations: Salaries, raw materials, manufacturing processes and equipment, offices and factories, consultants, lawyers, advertising, shipping, utilities etc. What is left over is the Net Income or Profit. Again: Revenues – Expenses = Net Income. "Your Income needs to be more than your Outflow or your Upkeep is your Downfall." My Mom used to say that. :)

Net income is either saved in order to smooth out future operations and deal with unforeseen events; or invested in new facilities, equipment, and technology. Or part of the profits can be paid out to the company owners, sometimes called **shareholders** or stockholders, as a **dividend**.

The Income Statement is also known as the "profit and loss statement" or "statement of revenue and expense." Business people sometimes use the shorthand term "**P&L**," which stands for profit and loss statement. A manager is said to have "P&L responsibilities" if they run an autonomous division where they make the decisions about marketing, sales, staffing, products, expenses, and strategy. **P & L responsibility** is one of the most important responsibilities of any executive position and involves monitoring the net income after expenses for a department or entire organization, with direct influence on how company resources are allocated.

The terms "profits," "earnings" and "net income" all mean the same thing and are used interchangeably.

Remember: Income (revenue or sales) – Expenses = Net Income or profit

Google the term "income statement" and you will see lots of examples of formats and presentations. You will see there is variety depending on the industry and nature of the business but they all follow these basic principles.

You can download my free ebook on Reading and Understanding Financial Statements on my website http://www.mba-asap.com

WHY DO NET LOSSES REDUCE RETAINED EARNINGS?

This question is a perfect one because it straddles the three financial statements and their impact on each other.

The impact of the Income Statement on the Balance Sheet is a great question that goes to the heart of accounting, financial statements, and financial reporting.

Net profits and net losses are recorded at the end of the period to the Balance Sheet in the Retained Earnings account. That is what retained earnings means. The bottom line of the Income Statement impacts the equity section of the Balance Sheet via Retained Earnings.

Below is a description of how accounting numbers flow through the three financial statements and how they are interconnected.

THE BIG PICTURE OF FINANCIAL STATEMENTS

The three Financial Statements: Balance Sheet, Income Statement, and Cash Flow Statement are interconnected, and the accounting numbers flow through them. They are the measure of a company's performance and health.

The interconnection starts with a Balance Sheet showing the financial position at the beginning of the period (usually a year); next, you have the Income Statement that shows the operations during the year, and then a Balance Sheet at the end of the year.

The Cash Flow Statement is necessary to **reconcile** the cash position starting from the Net Income number at the bottom of the Income Statement.

The cash number calculated from the Cash Flow Statement is added to the cash reported on the beginning Balance Sheet in the Cash account. This number needs to match the actual money in the bank at the end of the period. These steps represent the reconciliation process where you reconcile the cash account number in your accounting software to the actual balance in your bank account.

The reconciled amount is recorded as the Cash account balance at the top right (Asset column) of the end of year (EOY) Balance Sheet.

The Net Income number from the Income Statement (profit or loss) is then added, or subtracted in the case of a loss, to the Retained Earnings number in the Equity section (lower left-hand side) of the end of year (EOY) Balance Sheet. *A profit increases retained earnings, and a loss decreases retained earnings. (This addresses your specific question.)*

Changes in non-cash accounts like Accounts Receivable and Accounts Payable and Depreciation and Amortization will make up the difference between the Cash Flow number added on the right side of the Balance Sheet and the Net Income number added on the left-hand side.

When these steps are performed correctly, all the numbers should reconcile. The Assets will be equal to the Liabilities and Equity (remember the Accounting Equation A = L + E) on the EOY Balance Sheet.

FINANCIAL STATEMENT INTERCONNECTIONS AND FLOW

Think of it as a system of two Balance Sheets acting as bookends for the Income Statement. The Cash Flow Statement reconciles the Net Income (or Loss) at the bottom of the Income Statement with the amount of cash actually in the bank.

This process accounts for every penny that has come in, gone through, and gone out of a company during the period.

Understanding the three financial statements and how they knit together will allow you to assess the financial health, viability, and prospects of any company, and help you make rational fact-based investment decisions. It's the basis of Value Investing, and this is how Warren Buffett does it.

This post ties together the functionality of the financial statements. I hope this might be an "aha" moment for you. It was for me when I finally realized how this all fit and worked together.

Understanding how to read and understand financial statements is the basis of Financial Literacy and Capitalism. Following this big conceptual picture of accounting will provide a context to keep you from ever getting lost in the details like specific debits and credits.

Suffice it to say one of the greatest thinkers and writers Johann Wolfgang von Goethe called double entry accounting "among the finest inventions of the human mind."

WHY MIGHT A COMPANY HIRE ONE BIG 4 ACCOUNTING FIRM OVER ANOTHER TO AUDIT ITS FINANCIAL STATEMENTS?

There are lots of very good accounting firms that offer corporate auditing services. The Big 4 have consolidated from what used to be called the Big 8. They are the largest accounting firms and have international operations. Choosing one over the other would come down to whether their offices overlap with a companies operations geographically, price, timing, and whether a CFO feels a comfortable relationship with the accountants handling the audit.

Here is more general information on the role of auditors and the process.

The Role of Auditors

As per the SEC requirements and regulations, in order to be eligible to be traded on a U.S. stock exchange, a publicly traded company's financials must be prepared by the company and then reviewed and audited by an outside Certified Public Accountant (CPA).

What is an auditor?

The auditing process entails reviewing the financial statements prepared and drafted by the company to make sure they conform to GAAP and other rules. The auditors also "test" the numbers by requesting and reviewing supporting documentation such as invoices, checks, bills, and contracts. They send letters to the company's banks to confirm bank balances and contact lawyers the company has worked with to confirm that there are no liabilities or lawsuits pending that have not been disclosed.

The Auditing Process

In a company, performance is paramount. There are strong temptations to commit fraud for personal gain or to make the numbers look better.

People who run companies have the power to exploit financial information for personal gain. For publicly traded companies annual auditing is a legal requirement. The investors of many privately held companies, including their bankers, also require annual audited financial statements.

The audit process is designed to protect against misrepresenting financial information to improve results, avoid taxation, hide fraud, or not report latent liabilities. Audits are a process of gaining information about the financial systems and the financial records of a company.

Financial audits are performed to ascertain the validity and reliability of information, as well as to provide an assessment of the company's internal control system. Audits are carried out by a third party impartial account that is certified as a CPA.

What does it take to be an auditor?

To work on other company's financials you must be a CPA. In the United States a CPA will have passed the Uniform Certified Public Accountant Examination and met additional state education and experience requirements for membership in their state's professional accounting body. You don't have to be a CPA to work for a company internally as an employee in accounting or finance. You can be a CFO and not be a CPA.

Since the auditor cannot feasibly know or discover everything about a company, an audit seeks to provide reasonable assurance that the financial statements are free from material error. Test work and sampling of documents is performed in audits as a way to statistically confirm that the company has done the accounting properly.

A set of financial statements is understood to be 'true and fair' when they are deemed free of material misstatements. The auditor confirms this in their opinion letter that precedes the financials in the presentation. The opinion given on financial statements depends on the audit evidence obtained. You find the opinion letter at the beginning of the audited financial statements.

You can review the audited financial statements of publicly traded companies on the SEC website under the EDGAR tab. Look for the company's most recent 10K filing.

WHAT HAPPENS WHEN AN EXTERNAL AUDITOR QUALIFIES A FINANCIAL STATEMENT WHICH DOES NOT COMPLY TO THE STANDARDS?

A company never wants to get a qualified opinion from their auditors. That means the company did not follow Generally Accepted Accounting Principals GAAP. It can mean poor controls and procedures for accounting, or fraud and cover-up. Its not a good situation.

If the company is publicly traded the regulators like the SEC can remove their listing. If the company is private then the investors, owners, creditors, banks, vendors and others involved with the company may stop doing business with the company or move to remove top management or sue.

A company's ability to keep good records and accounting is critical to maintaining confidence in its ability to operate well.

BY ADOPTING THE COST ACCOUNTING METHOD, CAN A FIRM PREPARE A FINANCIAL STATEMENT?

The short answer is financial statements are not derived from cost accounting accounts.

Cost accounting and financial accounting have different audiences.

Cost accounting is an internal activity for managers. Cost accounting focuses on measuring direct and indirect costs.

What gets measured gets managed, so measure what matters.

Cost accounting measures manufacturing and inventory as Work In Progress (WIP) though all its progressive stages.

This information is proprietary and strategic and not shared with the outside world.

Financial accounting used different accounts. Its end product is the preparation of financial statements.

Financial Statements are for external audiences that have an interest in the company.

Financial statements provide information on the performance of the company. Interested parties are investors, creditors, government agencies, vendors, and others.

It's the same numbers sliced and diced in different ways to meet different ends.

WHAT ARE MONTHLY FIXED COSTS AND UNIT VARIABLE COSTS?

Fixed costs are the costs incurred no matter how many units you sell. For example a Pizzeria needs an oven no matter if it sells zero pizzas or 1,000. Monthly fixed costs are all those costs for the month, or annual costs divided by 12.

Variable costs are the cost of the things that go into the product or service. For a pizza it would be the dough, sauce, and labor to make it. Each pizza is a unit. These costs are a function of how many units you make.

Your total costs are your fixed costs plus your variable costs.

CAN AVERAGE FIXED COST BE ZERO?

There are two kinds of costs in a cost structure: fixed and variable. If all the costs of a product or service are variable, then fixed costs could conceivably by zero. With digital products delivered via the internet the fixed costs can be very small.

HOW DO YOU KNOW IF THE ASSETS LISTED IN THE BALANCE SHEET SHOW THE REAL VALUE?

The assets listed on a balance sheet don't show their current market value. Assets are initially recorded at cost. Then, each year, their cost value is reduced by the depreciation recorded for that year.

For example, if a machine cost $100,000 it will be recorded at $100,000. Then the accountant for the company will estimate its useful life. Say that is 5 years. So each year $20,000 worth of its value will be recorded as an expense in the Income Statement. And that $20,000 will be subtracted from the purchase price on the Balance Sheet as accumulated depreciation. So, its "value" on the Balance Sheet is now $80,000.

The next year another $20,000 is recorded and now the value is $60,000. It is the original cost less accumulated depreciation.

After five years the asset is worth zero on the books even though it may be used for another ten years.

This process shows the difference between the book value of assets and their market value.

————

FINANCIAL STATEMENTS

WHAT IS THE DEFINITION OF THE TERMS FINANCIAL STATEMENT?

What are financial statements?

There are 3 Financial Statements: Balance Sheet, Income Statement, and Cash Flow Statement. They are the reports that accounting produces. Financial Statements are the end product of accounting.

Financial Statements are the primary language of money and business. Everyone should have a basic understanding of Financial Statements: what they are and what information they provide. It's a competency that can open up opportunities and vistas that are closed off otherwise.

Executives in a company like the CEO, COO, and CFO routinely share and discuss financial data with marketing, operations, and other direct reports and personnel. They also compile and share financial information with stakeholders outside the firm, such as bankers, investors, and the media.

But most people don't understand finance and the numbers. A recent investigation into this question concluded that even most managers and employees don't understand enough to be useful.

THREE MAIN FINANCIAL STATEMENTS

There are three main financial statements, and they are linked together to provide a picture of an enterprise's financial position and health. They represent the end product of accounting, meaning they are the reports generated by accounting covering all of a company's transactions.

The three primary financial statements are the

- **Balance Sheet**: which shows firm's assets, liabilities, and net worth on a stated date
- **Income Statement**: also called profit & loss statement or simply the P&L: which shows how the net income of the firm is arrived at over a stated period, and
- **Cash Flow Statement**: This shows the inflows and outflows of cash due to the firm's activities during a stated period.

Knowing how to read and understand financial statements is a business skill you can't ignore. It can help work your way up the corporate ladder by communicating with others in your company and understanding the big picture. It is also a useful skill to know where your efforts and work can make the most impact.

When you are thinking about possibly changing jobs and working for a company, you can check their financials and make sure they are healthy. If you are considering starting your own company, you will need to have financials prepared by your accountant to talk to investors, bankers, and vendors.

Suppose you want to invest wisely in the stock market, analyze the competition, or benchmark your performance. In that case, you can look up any publicly-traded company's financials at the Securities and Exchange Commission website's' EDGAR filings and get an idea of how they are doing. Check out any public company's most recent 10K filing there. A 10K is the Annual Report of the company and its most important business and financial disclosure document.

WHAT IS THE BALANCE SHEET EQUATION?

The Balance Sheet can be summarized as: **Assets = Liabilities + Equity**. This is called the accounting equation; memorize it. These three *balance sheet* segments give the interested reader an idea as to what a company owns (**assets**) and owes (**liabilities**), and the amount invested and accumulated by the owners or shareholders (**equity**).

The Balance Sheet is a snapshot of the financial position of a company at a particular point in time. It is compiled at the end of the year or quarter. It is a summary of the Assets, Liabilities and Equity.

Think of how your home is financed as simple balance sheet. The **asset** is the value of the house. This is determined by an appraisal or sale. The value of your home varies as the market varies. An appraiser takes into account recent sales in the area and adjusts for differences like an extra bedroom or bathroom. An appraisal also takes into account replacement value; how much would it cost to recreate the house with the current costs for materials and labor. The **liability** is the **mortgage** balance and the **equity** (in this case we call it the home-owner's equity) is the difference between the two.

If the house is worth more than you owe, then you have positive equity. If the mortgage balance is more than the value of the home, then you have negative equity, sometimes called being "upside down" or "underwater".

The same concepts apply to a corporate balance sheet. If the assets are greater than the liabilities then there is positive shareholder's equity. If the liabilities are more than the assets, the company is considered **insolvent**. In this case a company declares bankruptcy.

BALANCE SHEET PRESENTATION

A Balance Sheet is constructed of two basic parts. Assets are listed in a column and totaled at the bottom of the column. Liabilities and Equity are listed in another column with the liabilities section listed above the equity section. Liabilities and Equity are each totaled separately and then together at the bottom. Sometimes these columns are presented in a stacked form with the Asset column on top. And sometimes these columns are presented side by side with the Assets on the left hand side and both Liabilities and Equity on the right hand side.

The Liabilities and Equity show how the Assets are financed. Liabilities and Equity totals in the right hand column must exactly equal the Asset total at the bottom of the left hand column.

When someone talks about the left hand side of the balance sheet, they are referring to assets; if they talk about the right hand side of the balance sheet, they mean liabilities and equity.

For comparison purposes, the Balance Sheet numbers of the previous year are also usually presented next to this year's numbers. Remember the goal of these Financial Statements is to present the financial information in a clear and meaningful way so interested parties can quickly grasp the performance and status of the enterprise.

According to GAAP, the U.S. accounting standard, assets and liabilities are listed in the order of their liquidity, from short term to long term, as you go down the items listed in each column. Cash is the most liquid asset so it is listed on the top left of the Balance Sheet. Long term debt comes after short term debts in the Liability column and Equity is listed below the Liabilities. Equity is listed below Liabilities because shareholders have a junior claim on the assets of the corporation. In case of a bankruptcy or liquidation of the company, the money collected from the sale of assets goes first to pay the lenders. Any residual money after the lenders are paid off is distributed to the shareholders.

Outsides the United States, the rest of the world presents balance sheet items in the reverse order, from least liquid on top to most liquid at the bottom. The International Accounting Standards are referred to as IAS.

HOW DO YOU CALCULATE THE BOOK VALUE ON A BALANCE SHEET?

The book value of assets is what is reported on the balance sheet. It is the cost of the asset less depreciation. Book value can be a misleading indicator of the value of an asset. The asset may have appreciated in value over the time it has been depreciated on the books. Real estate is a good example.

HOW DO YOU ACQUIRE LEVERAGE?

Leverage is a fancy word for borrowing. Debt is leverage. Leverage is how one buys a house for only 20% equity. Leverage in a business is how much debt is used relative to equity for purchasing assets. It is the right-hand side of the balance sheet.

You usually acquire leverage from a bank in the form of a loan. The bank does credit analysis to gauge whether you can repay the loan. Default is the bank's biggest risk. That means you need to show steady historical income streams that can support the loan payments.

The amount of the income streams relative to the loan payments is called the debt service coverage ratio DSCR.

HOW CAN I CALCULATE THE STOCK VALUE OF MY BUSINESS?

Stock is the value of equity. They are synonyms. It is a balance sheet value. Assets = Liabilities + Equity. So Equity = Assets - Liabilities. That is the value of your stock.

WHAT DO NEGATIVE RETAINED EARNINGS MEAN ON THE BALANCE SHEET?

Negative retained earnings on the Balance Sheet means the company has been reporting net losses on the Income Statement and has chewed through all its equity.

In this situation, the Assets of the company are worth less than its debt and obligations.

It's a situation similar to if you own a house and the appraised value of the house is less than the mortgage.

` The company, like the house, is under water.

WHAT MAKES A BALANCE SHEET GOOD OR BAD?

The basic measure of the health of a Balance Sheet is whether the value of Assets is greater than Liabilities. The Accounting Equation is:

$$Assets = Liabilities + Equity$$

Shareholders or owners of a company essentially own the Equity. Equity has a positive value if Liabilities are less than Assets.

Think of a Balance Sheet like owning a home. The Asset value is set by an appraisal. The Liability is the mortgage. The Equity in the home is the difference between the two.

HOW DO YOU INCREASE CAPITAL ON A BALANCE SHEET?

A company increases its capital in two ways. It either **1)** makes an operating profit through net income and cash flow, or **2)** it takes on financing by either selling stock or taking on debt.

This increase in cash will show up on the balance sheet as an asset in the cash category. The offsetting entry will be to equity if it is from selling stock, a liability if it is from debt, or retained earnings if it is from operating earnings as profit.

———

FINANCIAL ANALYSIS

HOW CAN A PERSON FROM A NON-FINANCE BACKGROUND LEARN FUNDAMENTAL ANALYSIS FOR VALUING COMPANIES?

The value of a company is essentially the estimate of the present value of its future cash flows.

The technique that is at the core of corporate finance is calculating the present value of future cash flows. That is a mouthful, but the basic gist is based on the time value of money and the idea that a company is essentially an entity that generates cash flows each year into the future. The trick is estimating those future cash flows and how much they might grow or shrink and what the risks are to realizing them.

This is where you have to polish your crystal ball and do some deep analysis of the business and its markets and competitors. All this information is compiled in a spreadsheet of financial projections and the bottom line future cash flows are discounted back to the present value at some determined discount rate. The discount rate takes into account what similar investments are commanding in the market and any and all risks specific to this particular enterprise or asset.

This technique of calculating the present value of a stream of cash flows becomes essential when trying to value start-ups that have no revenue history or assets, or companies that are predicted to grow rapidly. In these cases you can't rely on past performance and history in order to come up with a value based on P/E or existing assets.

This is the technique favored by investment bankers, venture capitalists, private equity, hedge funds, and savvy investors, banks and credit analysts, and CFOs. It's not difficult to understand and you will be amazed how useful and powerful it can be.

FINANCIAL STATEMENT ANALYSIS: WHAT CHARACTERISTICS DOES A HEALTHY BALANCE SHEET HAVE?

A good balance sheet conveys the information in a clear and transparent manner.

The Balance Sheet is a condensed statement that shows the financial position of an entity on a specified date, usually the last day of an accounting period.

Among other items of information, a balance sheet states

- What Assets the entity owns,
- How it paid for them,
- What it owes (its Liabilities), and
- What is the amount left after satisfying the liabilities (its Equity)

Balance sheet data is based on what is known as the Accounting Equation: Assets = Liabilities + Owners' Equity.

Think of a Balance Sheet in terms related to everyday life. Home ownership, when you have a mortgage, is represented as a Balance sheet. Your home ownership basically has the three components of Asset, Liability and Equity. The Asset is the value of the house. This is determined by an appraisal. An appraisal takes into account recent sales of homes in the area and compensates for differences like the number of bath or bedrooms, the size of the lot, etc.

The Liability is the mortgage. This is how much you owe against the house. The Equity is the difference between the value of the Asset and the amount of the Liability. If your home is worth $200,000 and you have a remaining mortgage balance of $150,000, then you have $50,000 in Equity. We sometimes call this homeowner's equity.

If your mortgage balance is more than the value of the home, then you are considered "upside down" or "under water". The same principle applies to a business: if the value of its Liabilities is more than the value of the Assets then the enterprise is insolvent and probably headed for bankruptcy.

A Balance Sheet is organized under subheadings such as current assets, fixed assets, current liabilities, Long-term Liabilities, and Equity With income statement and cash flow statement, it comprises the financial statements; a set of documents indispensable in running a business.

HOW DO I FIND WHETHER A COMPANY IS FUNDAMENTALLY GOOD OR NOT?

The Graham and Dodd approach is referred to as Fundamental Analysis and includes: Economic analysis; Industry analysis; and Company analysis. Company Analysis is the primary realm of financial statement analysis. On the basis of these three analyses the value of the security is determined. Fundamental analysis is how bankers, analysts, and investors make long-term investment decisions.

WHAT ARE THE "BALANCE SHEET RATIOS" USED IN FINANCIAL STATEMENT ANALYSIS?

Financial ratios are powerful tools used to assess company upside, downside, and risk.

There are four main categories of financial ratios: liquidity ratios, profitability ratios, activity ratios, and leverage ratios. These are typically analyzed over time and across competitors in an industry.

Using ratios "normalizes" the numbers so you can compare companies in apples-to-apples terms.

Ratios compare numbers reported on the Balance Sheet and the Income Statement.

LIQUIDITY AND SOLVENCY

Solvency and liquidity are both refer to a company's financial health and viability. Solvency refers to an enterprise's capacity to meet its long-term financial commitments. Liquidity refers to an enterprise's ability to pay short-term obligations. Liquidity is also a measure of how quickly assets can be converted to cash by being sold.

A solvent company is one that owns more than it owes. It has a positive net worth and is carrying a manageable debt load. A company with adequate liquidity may have enough cash available to pay its bills, but may still be heading for financial disaster down the road. In this case, a company meets liquidity standards but is not solvent.

Healthy companies are both solvent and possess adequate liquidity.

Liquidity ratios determine whether a company has enough current asset capacity to pay its bills and meet its obligations in the foreseeable future (current liabilities).

Solvency ratios are a measure of how quickly a company can turn its assets into cash if it experiences financial difficulties or bankruptcy.

Liquidity and Solvency ratios measure different aspects of whether or not a company can pay its bills and remain in business.

The current ratio and the quick ratio are two common liquidity ratios. The **current ratio** is current assets/current liabilities and measures how much liquidity (cash) is available to address current liabilities (bills and other obligations). The **quick ratio** is (current assets – inventories) / current liabilities.

The quick ratio measures a company's ability to meet its short-term obligations based on its most liquid assets and therefore excludes inventories from its current assets. It is also known as the "acid-test ratio."

The **solvency ratio** examines the ability of a business to meet its long-term obligations. Lenders and bankers commonly review solvency. The ratio compares cash flows to liabilities. The solvency ratio calculation involves the following steps:

All non-cash expenses are added back to after-tax net income. This approximates the amount of cash flow generated by the business. You can find the numbers to add back in the Operations section of the Cash Flow Statement.

Add together all short-term and long-term obligations. This summation is the Total Liabilities number on the Balance Sheet. Then divide the estimated cash flow figure by the liabilities total.

The formula for the ratio is:

(Net after-tax income + Non-cash expenses)/(Short-term liabilities + Long-term liabilities)

A higher percentage indicates an increased ability to support the liabilities of the enterprise over the long-term.

Remember that estimations made over the long term are inherently inaccurate. Many variables can impact the ability to pay in the long run. Using any ratio used to estimate solvency is subject to a degree of uncertainty.

PROFITABILITY RATIOS

Profitability ratios are ratios that help discern how profitable a company is. To be profitable, a company has to cover costs. The breakeven point and the gross profit ratio address the dynamics of cost coverage in different ways.

The breakeven point calculates how much cash a company must generate to break even with their operating costs.

The gross profit ratio is equal to (revenue - the cost of goods sold)/revenue. This ratio provides a quick snapshot of expected revenue that can cover the overhead expenses and fixed costs of operations.

Some additional examples of profitability ratios are profit margin, return on assets, and return on Equity. The higher the value in these ratios, the more profitable a company is. Having a higher value relative to a competitor's ratio, or the same ratio from a previous period, is indicative that the company is performing relatively well and going in the right direction.

Return on Equity

Return on Equity (ROE) = Net Income / Average Shareholders' Equity

Earnings per Share

Earnings per share (EPS) is the portion of the company's profit, which is allocated to each outstanding share of common stock.

Earnings per share is an excellent indicator of the profitability of any organization, and it is one of the most widely used measures of profitability.

Activity ratios

Activity ratios show how well management is doing managing the company's resources. Activity ratios measure company sales relative to another asset account.

The most common asset accounts used are accounts receivable, inventory, and total assets. Since most companies have a lot of resources tied up in accounts receivable, inventory, and working capital, these accounts are in the denominator of the most common activity ratios.

Accounts receivable (AR) is the total amount of money due to a company for products or services sold on a credit account. The length of time until AR is collected is critical. A company must finance that expected revenue in some way. You can't pay bills with AR.

The accounts receivable turnover shows how rapidly a company collects what is owed to it and indicates the liquidity of the receivables.

Accounts Receivable Turnover = Total Credit Sales/Average Accounts Receivable

The average collection period in days is equal to 365 days, divided by the Accounts Receivable Turnover.

Another ratio that helps gain insight into AR collection is:

Average Collection Period = 365 Days/Accounts Receivable Turnover

Analysts frequently use the average collection period to measure the effectiveness of a company's ability to collect payments from its credit customers. The average collection period should be less than the credit terms that the company extends to its customers.

A significant indicator of profitability is the ability to manage inventory. Inventory is money and resources invested that do not earn a return until the product is sold.

The longer inventory sits, the less profitable a company can be. A higher inventory turnover ratio indicates more demand for products, better cash management, and also a reduced risk of inventory obsolescence.

The best measure of inventory utilization is the **inventory turnover ratio**. You calculate it as either the total annual sales or the cost of goods sold (COGS), divided by the cost of inventory.

Inventory Turnover = Total Annual Sales or Cost of Goods Sold/Average Inventory

Using the cost of goods sold in the numerator can provide a more accurate indicator of inventory turnover because it allows a more direct comparison with other companies. Different companies have different markups to the sale price, and this can obscure apples-to-apples comparison.

The average inventory cost is usually used in the denominator to compensate for seasonal differences.

LEVERAGE RATIOS

Leverage ratios analyze the degree to which a company uses debt to finance its operations and assets. The debt-to-equity ratio is the most common. You calculate this ratio as:

(Long-term debt + Short-term debt + Leases) / Equity

Companies with high debt ratios need to have steady and predictable revenue streams to service that debt. Companies whose revenues fluctuate and are less predictable should rely more on Equity in its capital structure. Leverage also has obvious implications for solvency.

Startups rely almost entirely on Equity as they have no revenues or very uncertain revenues that can service debt.

DUPONT ANALYSIS

The DuPont Corporation developed DuPont analysis in the 1920s as a tool to assess their investments across their various companies and operations. As a conglomerate, they need a tool to evaluate the relative performance of their different business units.

Dupont analysis is a tool to make decisions about where and how to allocate resources. It has become a widely adopted managerial and investment tool.

What drives ROE?

DuPont Analysis analyzes Return on Equity by deconstructing it into its main drivers.

DuPont Analysis is an expression, which breaks return on Equity (ROE) into three parts.

The basic formula is:

ROE = (Profit margin)*(Asset turnover)*(Equity multiplier) =

(Net   Income/Sales)*(Sales/Assets)*(Assets/Equity)   =   (Net Income/Equity)

The three constituent parts are:

- Profitability: measured by profit margin
- Operating efficiency: measured by asset turnover
- Financial leverage: measured by equity multiplier

DuPont analysis enables you to understand the source of superior (or inferior) return by comparison with companies in similar industries or between industries. It also provides a deeper level of understanding by parsing apart the significant variables and drivers of Return on Equity. And ROE is undoubtedly a metric that equity investors (stock investors) find essential.

Summary

Financial ratios are powerful tools. Use them to assess company upside, downside, and risk when you are evaluating stock investments.

There are four main categories of financial ratios:

·Liquidity ratios,

·Profitability ratios,

·Activity ratios,

·Leverage ratios.

These are typically analyzed over time and across competitors in an industry.

Ratios "normalize" the numbers so you can compare companies in apples-to-apples terms.

IS IT POSSIBLE TO CALCULATE ROUGHLY HOW MUCH HAS BEEN INVESTED IN A COMPANY IN TERMS OF THE SUM OF ALL PRICES PAID FOR ITS CURRENTLY OWNED STOCK? MARKET CAP ISN'T THE ANSWER, THAT IS THE CURRENT PRICE * NUMBER OF SHARES, NOT THE AMOUNT INVESTED.

Look at the Equity section of the Balance Sheet. There are three parts to the equity section:

- Par Value
- Additional Paid In Capital (APIC)
- Retained Earnings

You want to look at Par and APIC together. Par is a way to keep track of all the shares issued. Par is an arbitrary number like one dollar or one cent. APIC is all the additional money that was invested in the company when shares were issued.

Retained Earnings is the cumulative amount that has been contributed to Equity by operations over the years. Each year the addition, or subtraction, to RE is the Net Income (or loss) less any dividends.

WHAT ARE A FEW REASONS THAT YOU WOULD INVEST IN A COMPANY WITH A HIGH PRICE TO EARNINGS RATIO?

Companies command high PEs when investors bid up the stock price because they believe the company has significant growth prospects for the future.

The value of a stock is basically the accumulated guesses of all the investors as to the present value of the stream of future earnings.

All the investors are doing this calculation, either in their head as a rough estimate, or with fancy spreadsheet models with lots of refined assumptions.

As a rough rule: high growth companies have high PE ratios and low growth companies have low PE ratios.

HOW DOES ONE VALUE A COMPANY? WHERE CAN I LEARN MORE ABOUT WHAT DETERMINES THAT VALUE? IS THERE A WAY TO DO BACK OF A NAPKIN CALCULATION (LOOK AT PUBLICLY KNOWN METRICS) AND ARRIVE AT A BALLPARK VALUE THAT IS DEPENDABLE?

Valuation is an estimate of something's worth. Something's worth can be set at auction where people bid and the highest bidder wins. But how do bidders know how much to bid and how much is too much?

The stock market is essentially an auction where investors place bids: how much they are willing to pay for a stock and asks: how much an investor is willing to sell for.

The book Barbarians at the Gates tells the story of the conglomerate RJR Nabisco and its sale to the highest bidder. The buyout firm KKR ultimately won with the highest bid and bought the company. All the bidding groups went through lots of machinations to uncover the value of all the assets and divisions of RJR Nabisco.

Valuation of companies and assets can seem mysterious; where do you even begin? How can you value a startup that doesn't even have any revenues yet?

There are essentially two basic techniques that are used in Valuation. One is ratio analysis of financial statements and the other is calculating the present value of future cash flows. Bankers, investors, financiers and entrepreneurs use these tools and techniques.

By ratio analysis we mean taking two numbers from financial statements and dividing one by the other. This technique is good for comparing different companies or the same company over time. This works well because it eliminates any relative size differences between the companies so you can compare apples to apples.

A particularly common valuation of companies done by ratio analysis is based on multiples of Earnings. The price/earnings ratio P/E is a way companies are compared based on their stock price relative to their earnings (also called net income or profit) in the most recently reported year. The earnings number is the bottom line of the Income Statement. This works well for comparing public companies that report these numbers. This technique can be used to value a private company by comparing its earnings and valuation range to an average of public reporting companies in similar industry sectors and markets. This ratio technique can be used based on a multiple of revenues, the top line of the Income Statement.

You can also value the Assets of a company from its Balance Sheet. Here you have to make adjustments for assets that have been depreciated and are reported as less valuable on the balance sheet, their book value, than their market value is. A company can be thought of as a bunch of income producing assets.

The second technique that is at the core of corporate finance is calculating the present value of future cash flows. That is a mouthful, and I will break down the methodology in some subsequent posts, but the basic gist is based on the time value of money and the idea that a company is essentially an entity that generates cash flows each year into the future. The trick is estimating those future cash flows and how much they might grow or shrink and what the risks are to realizing them.

This is where you have to polish your crystal ball and do some deep analysis of the business and its markets and competitors. All this information is compiled in a spreadsheet of financial projections and the bottom-line future cash flows are discounted back to the present value at some determined discount rate that takes what similar investments are commanding in the market and any and all risks specific to this particular enterprise or asset.

This technique of calculating the present value of a stream of cash flows becomes essential when trying to value start-ups that have no revenue history or assets, or companies that are predicted to grow rapidly. In these cases, you can't rely on past performance and history in order to come up with a value based on P/E or existing assets.

This is the technique favored by investment bankers, venture capitalists, private equity, hedge funds, and savvy investors, banks and credit analysts, and CFOs. I will go into detail on this powerful tool in subsequent blog posts. It's not difficult to understand and you will be amazed how useful and powerful it can be.

HOW DO YOU ASSESS WHETHER A COMPANY'S DEBT LOAD IS TOO RISKY?

Basic credit analysis is a place to start. Analyze how robust and steady the revenues are. Are there lots of customers? Are there long-term contracts in place? Do they have a long operating history? Then analyze net income. Is it stable and growing?

Then look at the debt obligations. Are there big payments coming due? Is there a crisis at maturity for paying back debt? What is the debt service coverage ratio DSCR? That is how much of net income is needed to service debt each month.

Has the debt been used to purchase long term productive income producing assets?

Less debt is better.

———

CORPORATE FINANCE

DO WE CONSIDER CAPITAL BUDGETING AS AN ACCOUNTING CONCEPT OR A FINANCIAL ONE, OR IS IT IN BETWEEN?

The capital budgeting process is a hybrid of accounting and finance. It is forward looking so it uses corporate finance techniques. And budgets are constructed using pro forma financial statements so it is part accounting.

Budgets are financial projections developed for a relatively short and predetermined period of time. Most budgets are prepared for the next year and divided into detailed monthly budgets. Budgets can be expected to be reasonably accurate because they represent estimates of relatively short time periods and because they rely on historical information about the company.

Budgets are created, reviewed, and approved and then used to measure the actual performance of the company each month. Did the company under or over perform relative to the budget? The differences between the actual accounting prepared at the end of the month and the budget amounts is called a Variance.

Variances are reviewed and discussed to see why some line items went over budget and why some may be significantly under budget. Budgets are developed using historical performance data, which means that they are relatively predictive of the levels at which a company should be operating. And the budget will reflect the goals that management hopes to achieve in the coming year.

Budgeting is part of the planning process and reviewing the actual results against the budget on a regular basis is good management practice.

WHEN A COMPANY'S AWARD SPECIAL DIVIDEND PAYMENTS, IS THAT EQUITY EXTRACTED FROM MARKET CAPITALIZATION?

Market capitalization is the value that investors place on a company through trading in its stock.

If a share of stock is trading at $10 per share and there are 100 million shares outstanding, then the company's market cap is $1 Billion.

Dividends are paid out of earnings. Earnings, Profit, and Net Income mean the same thing; they are synonymous. Earnings, net of dividends, are plowed into the Retained Earnings section of Equity on the Balance Sheet.

So, the amount that gets put into Retained Earnings at the end of the year is less by the amount paid out to shareholders as a dividend.

The accounting book value of the company and the market cap are independent of each other.

HOW DO YOU ESTIMATE THE AGGREGATE VALUE OF PRIVATE COMPANIES?

If you are selling or acquiring a company, then the value will ultimately be determined by negotiation. To support the ask and offer there will two methods of valuation:

Valuing the assets: how much each asset is worth in the market.

Present Value of future cash flows: an estimate of the future cash flows discounted back to the present. Picking a discount rate and estimating future revenues and costs etc. requires a number of assumptions that can be challenged and must be agreed upon.

If you want more information on discounting cash flows and present value calculations, check out my book on corporate finance.

WHAT'S THE REASON A COMPANY DOESN'T WANT TO GO PUBLIC?

Highly functioning public equity markets are one of the two greatest economic innovations of the twentieth century. The other is the corporate form of organization. Together these two forces have driven economic development and rising standards of living.

There was a time when the public markets were the only vehicle for raising large sums of money for growing enterprises. Now there are alternative sources of significant capital.

There are many companies these days that have surpassed a billion dollars valuation without being publicly traded. Private Equity is a thriving investment segment where public companies are acquired and taken private. The idea here is to unleash latent value that the public market was underpricing.

These are two examples of industry segments that do not rely on public markets for pricing or funding.

Going public via an IPO is an expensive and time consuming proposition. Once a company is public there are burdens of reporting that require staff and auditors. A lot of information about the company and its operations must be disclosed. That information disclosure can compromise some competitive advantage.

Investors are quick to punish a public company by selling its stock if it doesn't meet quarterly expectations. This can detract from long term strategic planning and put an emphasis on short term expediency in operations.

I took two companies public and was a public company CEO and CFO for almost two decades. I also took one of those companies private again.

Going public is the right choice under certain circumstances. Staying private has advantages under other sets of circumstance. It's about choosing the right tool for the right job.

HOW MANY INDUSTRIES ARE THERE IN THE WORLD? HOW CAN I GET TRUSTFUL SOURCES THAT UPDATES ABOUT THIS?

The standard industry classification SIC system is a good place to look. Every publicly traded company lists their SIC on the front page of their 10K so you can tell in which industry they consider themselves primarily operating.

SIC is a system for classifying industries by a four-digit code. It was established in the U. S. in 1937. It is used by government agencies and corporations to classify industry areas. The SIC system is also used by agencies in other countries such as the U.K.

HOW DOES A COMPANY BENEFIT FROM A LOW STOCK PRICE?

I can't think of any benefits that can accrue to a company from a low stock price. Low and high are relative terms and have to do with investor's perception of the company's prospects to grow and make profits in the future. The stock price is essentially the cumulative estimate of the present value of the future cash flows of the company. A low stock price means that investors don't think too highly of the company's prospects going forward.

———

LEVEL UP!

For more business skills and knowledge check out www.mba-asap.com and sign up for the our newsletter!

THANK YOU FOR READING!

Dear Reader,

I hope you enjoyed *Financial Statements A$AP* and found it filled with useful and valuable information..

As an author, I love feedback. Candidly, you are the reason that I organize my thoughts, write, and explore these topics. So, tell me what you liked, what was helpful and what could be better explained or left out. You can write me at john@mba-asap.com and visit me on the web at www.mba-asap.com.

Finally, I need to ask a favor. I'd love a review on Amazon of *Financial Statements A$AP*. I'd just appreciate your feedback.

Reviews can be tough to come by these days. You, the reader, have the power now to make or break a book. If you have the time, here's a link to my author page on Amazon where you can find all of my books: https://www.amazon.com/-/e/B01JVF2XTU or just search for the title and my name on Amazon. A quick review will be immensely appreciated!

Thank you so much for reading *Financial Statements A$AP* and for spending the time and effort with me.

In deep gratitude,

John Cousins

ABOUT THE AUTHOR

John Cousins (@jjcousins) is an investor, tech founder, and bestselling author of Understanding Corporate Finance and over 40 other books.

John is the founder of MBA ASAP, which provides training to individuals and corporations including Adidas, Apple, General Mills, Kaiser Permanente, Lyft, PayPal, Pinterest, Mercedes-Benz, and Volkswagen.

John has taught MBA students at universities worldwide.

Currently General Partner at Tetraktys Global, a quantitative hedge fund, he is an early investor in many successful tech companies and crypto protocols, including Databricks, SpaceX, Anthropic, Discord, Udemy, Coursera, Fastly, UiPath, Palantir, Bitcoin, Chainlink, Ethereum, and Solana.

John was the cofounder of Biomoda (IPO 2006), Advanced Optics Electronics (IPO 1999), FoodSentry (epic fail), MBA ASAP, and Tetraktys Global. He holds undergraduate degrees from MIT and Boston University and an MBA in finance from Wharton.

———

 X

Made in United States
Troutdale, OR
01/01/2025

27472593R00080